Cambridge Elements ≡

Elements in Shakespeare Performance
edited by
W. B. Worthen
Barnard College

THIS DISTRACTED GLOBE

Attending to Distraction in Shakespeare's Theatre

Jennifer J. Edwards
The Queen's College, Oxford

CAMBRIDGE
UNIVERSITY PRESS

Shaftesbury Road, Cambridge CB2 8EA, United Kingdom

One Liberty Plaza, 20th Floor, New York, NY 10006, USA

477 Williamstown Road, Port Melbourne, VIC 3207, Australia

314–321, 3rd Floor, Plot 3, Splendor Forum, Jasola District Centre,
New Delhi – 110025, India

103 Penang Road, #05–06/07, Visioncrest Commercial, Singapore 238467

Cambridge University Press is part of Cambridge University Press & Assessment,
a department of the University of Cambridge.

We share the University's mission to contribute to society through the pursuit of
education, learning and research at the highest international levels of excellence.

www.cambridge.org
Information on this title: www.cambridge.org/9781108969901

DOI: 10.1017/9781108979986

First published 2023

A catalogue record for this publication is available from the British Library.

ISBN 978-1-108-96990-1 Paperback
ISSN 2516-0117 (online)
ISSN 2516-0109 (print)

This Distracted Globe

Attending to Distraction in Shakespeare's Theatre

Elements in Shakespeare Performance

DOI: 10.1017/9781108979986
First published online: May 2023

Jennifer J. Edwards
The Queen's College, Oxford

Author for correspondence: Jennifer J. Edwards, jennifer.edwards@queens.ox.ac.uk

ABSTRACT: This Element attends to attention drawn away. That the Globe is a 'distracted' space is a sentiment common to both *Hamlet*'s original audience and attendees at the reconstructed theatre on London's Bankside. But what role does distraction play in this modern performance space? What do attitudes to 'distraction' reveal about how this theatre space asks and invites us to pay attention? Drawing on scholarly research, artist experience, and audience behaviour, *This Distracted Globe* considers the disruptive, affective, phenomenological, and generative potential of distraction in contemporary performance at the Globe.

KEYWORDS: attention, distraction, Shakespeare, performance, theatre, affect

ISBNs: 9781108969901 (PB), 9781108979986 (OC)
ISSNs: 2516-0117 (online), 2516-0109 (print)

Contents

Introduction

'You have to put up with a lot of distractions at the Globe: the mercurial weather, the officious ushers, the restless crowd' (Billington, 2000). This Element begins, as this project began, with the opening sentiment from Michael Billington's review of *Hamlet* in 2000, which echoes Hamlet's famous line 'whiles memory holds a seat │ In this distracted globe' (I.v.96–7).[1] It is, perhaps, a negative note to start on: distraction gets a lot of bad press, as Billington's use of the term here exemplifies; 'it's hard to focus on "To be or not to be"', he continues, 'when some Yankee tourist is wrestling with his crinkly Pac-a-mac. But it says a lot for Mark Rylance's performance and Giles Block's production that they overcome the countless obstacles built into playgoing at the Globe.' Distraction is so often seen as the bad twin of attention; it pulls away from the more valuable thing that we are told and encouraged to pay, taught how to manage and maintain, and cautioned against losing. Distractions, as Billington has it, are 'obstacles' that 'you have to put up with' in this space. As I will argue in what follows, however, attending at the Globe is not something to which distraction is anathema but, rather, an intrinsic aspect of this particular theatregoing experience.

What exactly Hamlet refers to when he describes 'this distracted globe' is not entirely clear. Ann Thompson and Neil Taylor offer three potential glosses of the line in the Arden Third Series edition of the text: '(1) while [my] memory has any power over my shattered frame; (2) while memory [in general] is a force in this disordered world. Yet a third meaning may have occurred to the first auditors at the Globe' (Shakespeare, 2016: 219).[2] The sense of a third meaning here – that is, 'globe' as in Globe theatre, in addition to the 'globe' of Hamlet's head, which is by extension perhaps a microcosm of a 'distracted' world – is, for

---

[1] Unless otherwise stated, references to Shakespeare are to *The Norton Shakespeare* (2016).

[2] *The Norton Shakespeare* (2016) similarly offers these three interpretations: 'Confused head; disordered world; often also taken as a reference to the Globe Theater and the audience' (1782n.). Karremann (2015) focusses on the last to inform a reading of memory and distraction in Shakespeare's history plays.

some, less certain. 'Despite the temptations to suppose otherwise,' writes Rhodri Lewis, 'there is no critical warrant or contextual evidence to support the claim that it has anything to do with the Globe Theatre' (Lewis, 2020: 163). For Lewis, a meta-theatrical pun at this moment 'not only shatters the metaphorical economy of the lines, but undermines the intensity and the integrity of the dramatic moment' (163). There is, however, something fitting about the idea of a reference to the Globe that meta-theatrically distracts from the drama, that momentarily draws attention from the stage to the surrounding building; there is something apt about a phrase like 'distracted globe' having the capacity to facilitate or create what it describes. Whether it was intended or not, this sense of a 'distracted Globe' has, as this Element will demonstrate, informed the new Globe's approach to rehearsal, performance, and even its response to the Covid-19 pandemic.[3] It is with this in mind that the present study gives distraction its full attention.

*

Since 2006, the Research department at the Globe has conducted end-of-season interviews (EoSIs) with the actors and creatives behind each production in the theatre's summer season.[4] These interviews run alongside, but are distinct from, the 'Ask an Actor' (formerly 'Adopt an Actor')

---

[3] While early modern works will at times inform what follows, this study is primarily interested in the role of distraction in the new Globe. As such, this Element builds on studies of Globe performances and audiences including Worthen (2003), Escolme (2005), Carson and Karim-Cooper (2008), Woods (2012), and Purcell (2013). For a comprehensive overview of and recent contributions to work on Shakespeare's audiences (old and new), see collections by Banks (2018) and Pangallo and Kirwan (2021). For studies of attention and distraction in the early modern Globe, see especially Dawson (2001), Tribble (2011), Lyne (2020), and West (2021).

[4] From 2015 to 2019 I oversaw this interview project as the Globe's Research Co-ordinator. As far as is possible, I have sought to ensure that my involvement does not compromise the critical insights that I offer here.

interviews that feature on the Globe's website.[5] Where the 'Ask/Adopt an Actor' interviews are public-facing, documenting an actor's experience working at the Globe from rehearsals through to performance, sometimes allowing members of the public to suggest questions or topics for discussion, the EoSIs take place towards the end of a production's run and follow an interview script that has remained largely consistent.[6] Roughly eleven questions serve as prompts for a conversation, lasting for around half an hour, about the performance conditions and technical requirements of playing at the Globe, from the transition between rehearsal room and the theatre to the design of the space, the relationship with the audience, and differences between matinee and evening shows. From 2009, intrigued by Billington's echoing of Hamlet's distracted g/Globe, these interviews asked specifically about responses to distraction in the space. Drawing on the testimonies of more than fifty actors and creatives who worked on productions at the Globe between 2006 and 2021, this Element suggests that reflections on and records of distraction unlock something about the particularities, challenges, and rewards of playing in this space. Analysis of this archive will be supported by reviews, front-of-house (FOH) show reports, personal interviews, and surveys, with an aim of bringing to light the value of attending to distraction in this theatre. In this, I share with Adam Phillips a sense that 'we might define an object by the distraction to which it leads' (2019: 110). For, as Michael Wood puts it when urging readers to tune into diversion, 'concentration has all kinds of virtues but also a strange gift for missing what distraction can find' (2009: 583). This is, in many ways, a guiding principle of what follows: that distraction can have value and utility, not simply detrimental effects. Even Billington (2000) seems to come round to this way of thinking, giving in to the Globe's distracting impulse and leaving his seat: 'It's a traditional production with an original central performance. But, as

---

[5] The 'Ask an Actor' interview archive is available at www.shakespearesglobe.com/ discover/ask-an-actor.

[6] For an analysis of the experiences of creatives and actors working in the indoor Sam Wanamaker Theatre, see Tosh (2018).

so often at the Globe, I found the play came most alive when I quit my assigned seat to roam around the yard: if you can't beat the distracting multitude, canoodling and flicking through their tourist guides, the only thing to do is to join them.'

Defining Distraction

Distraction is attention   drawn away.

Where attention stretches out (from the Latin *adtendĕre*, to stretch), distraction (from the Latin *distrahĕre*, to pull or drag apart) frays, draws asunder, disrupts. Attention connects; distraction fractures, throws us off track. In a now obsolete meaning, distraction once signalled a kind of violent stretching or extension: almost a kind of attentive stretching in excess.[7] As critics have recently discussed, distraction is not necessarily the opposite of attention but rather a form of it, a kind of attention attracted elsewhere, dis- or misplaced. 'Attention', Matthew Bevis notes, 'could be conceived of as the sublimation of distraction, not its opposite' (2017: 180). Common to both words is a sense of being pulled: attention towards, distraction away. The latter is not an exclusively negative phenomenon: in French, we might be *divertissement*, pleasurably diverted or entertained (OED, *n.* 1); a wandering or distracted mind may bring about relaxation (OED, distraction, *n.* 2a); for birds, 'distraction flights' are useful diverting displays that serve to draw a predator's attention away from offspring in the nest (OED, distraction, *n.* 2 c).[8] But distraction is hard to capture, and to attend to it seems paradoxical; as Paul North explains, 'as a tendency towards the limit of what is, distraction is nearest when it escapes notice and most remote when attended to' (2012: 13). We become aware of distraction after the fact: wondering what it was we were just thinking

---

[7] The Oxford English Dictionary (OED) offers an example from 1737 of 'Fibres . . . in a State of Distraction, that is, they are drawn out into a greater Length' – 'distraction', *n.* d. (OED Online, accessed 15 March 2023).

[8] See Anne Stillman (2012) for a reading of these distracted flights as a model for thinking through T. S. Eliot's poems.

about, finding we need to read a paragraph again because we were not focussing properly the first time. Distraction has the tendency to create gaps in our attention without our knowing it. The same is in some ways true of attention, which we likewise tend to account for belatedly: 'we can never truly say "I am absorbed"', as Bevis notes (2017: 191). Here distinctions blur. We can lose ourselves in both. Is distraction a mind temporarily suspended, or might that be a description of deep attention? Can we attend to multiple things at once, or is fractured focus more properly a variety of distraction? Yet a near constant remains that we attribute to one a positive value while we denigrate the other. We give or pay attention; we are subject to distraction.

Before turning to issues of performance, let us first detour through distraction. For early moderns, this was a term that encompassed both risk and opportunity, the perilous and the pleasurable. As Carol Thomas Neely explores in *Distracted Subjects*, 'in the early modern period, "distract" was a common symptom of and name for extreme cases of mental disorder' (2004: 2–3).

Enter Ophelia, distracted.

In these circumstances, the distracted subject is one whose mind is scattered, dangerously diverted in a 'madding fever', as it is in Shakespeare's 'Sonnet 119' (l. 8). Elsewhere, 'distract' is used as a synonym for all kinds of fracture or division, from the geographic – 'Africa is more uniform and spacious; but Europe is of a more distracted and manifold shape, being in sundry places dispersed and restrained by the sea' (Leo, 1600: 2) – to the geopolitical: 'countries distract he doth to Union bring' (Mason, 1605: 110).[9] The real peril of distraction, however, is its potential to draw away from God the early modern subject, who should 'Attend upon the Lord without distraction' (1 Corinthians 7: 35 King James Version). It is in these circumstances that we find recommendations for readings to focus the mind into devotional meditation – 'when thy heart is ... distracted, that it can not enter into prayer, then mayest thou stay somewhat the longer in reading, or join meditation and reading together' (Granada, 1582: 284) – as well as those

---

[9] Note that all early modern spellings have been modernised.

who complain that 'long prayers are often performed with much negligence, and subject to the interruptions and distractions of worldly cogitations and wandering thoughts' (Downame, 1622: 231–2). '[F]orgive me, though I have other things in my mind when I pray besides thee', reads *Of the Imitation of Christ* (à Kempis, 1580): 'For, to say the truth, I am wont greatly to be distracted; and many times there am I not, where bodily I sit, or stand, but whether my cogitations carry me' (233). So far, so gloomy. But beneath these repeated warnings that 'the mind . . . should be wholly intent to Gods worship', indeed what drives them, is a recognition of the capacity for the mind to be 'distracted and lead away to pleasures' (Widley, 1604: 109). Reading, in these terms, is figured not only as a way of focussing a distracted mind towards prayer but as a 'delectable distraction' in its own right (Petrarch, 1579: 62). There is pleasure at the limits of attention.

Where Rogers sought forgiveness for the wandering of his mind, French philosopher Michel de Montaigne celebrates diversion, building it into his essayistic method: 'Even in my writings, I shall not at all times find the track', he explains. 'I do but come and go; my judgement doth not always go forward, but is ever floating, and wandering': 'where I incline, there I entertain myself, howsoever it be, and am carried away by mine own weight' (1603: II.12.329).[10] Adopting what Anne Cotterill has described as 'the narrative practice of stepping away' (2004: 6), Montaigne weaves quotations through his prose, meanders attention through one textual digression after another, all the while openly acknowledging his tendency to 'straggle out of the path' (Montaigne, 1603: III.9.595). 'Yet', he explains, 'it is rather by licence, than by unadvisedness: My fantasies follow one another: but sometimes a far-off, and look one at another; but with an oblique look' (595). Characteristically, Montaigne approaches his topics not straight-on but sidewards, obliquely: essayistic attention is paid not linearly

---

[10] In characteristically contradictory terms, we find elsewhere in the *Essais* denials of distraction: 'But to affections that distract me from my selfe, and divert me elsewhere; surely, to such I oppose myself with all my force' (Montaigne, 1603: III.10.600).

but at a slight angle. 'We ever think on somewhat else' (III.4.501), he notes in his essay 'Of Diversions', willingly giving himself over to the detour; after all, he suggests, 'a little thing doth divert and turn us; for a small thing holds us' (III.4.503). This kind of 'digressing and diverting' (500) is not exclusive to Montaigne's attention but is, he suggests, 'in all things else': 'nature proceedth thus, by the benefit of inconstancy', of 'shifting of place' (502). 'When physicians cannot purge the rheum,' he explains,

> they divert and remove the same unto some less dangerous part. I also perceive it to be the most ordinary receite [remedy] for the mind's diseases. . . . *Our mind also is some-times to be diverted to other studies, cogitations, cares, and business: and lastly to be cured by chance of place, as sick folks use, that otherwise cannot get health.* One makes it seldom to shock mischiefs with direct resistance; one makes it neither bear nor break, but shun or divert the blow. (500)[11]

From 'public diversions' to 'ingenious diverting', Montaigne describes the positive, sometimes curative potential of distraction, of 'declining our discourses, and by degrees bending them unto [other] subjects' (499–500). As with the magician's diversion or a bird's distracted flight, there is utility in the detour of attention, the digressive diversion, the essayistic swerve. On this matter, a writer such as John Dryden would agree: '[Plutarch] was more happy in his digressions than any we have named. I have always been pleased to see him, and his imitator, *Montaign*, when they strike a little out of the common road: For we are sure to be the better for their wandering' (Dryden, 1683: 98).

Moving to the present moment, issues of attention and distraction have felt increasingly timely during the period of writing this Element. During

---

[11] Elsewhere, Montaigne continues to signal the curative potential of such diversions: 'Whoso will sequester or distract his mind, let him hardily do it, if he can, at what time his body is not well at ease, thereby to discharge it from that contagion' (Montaigne, 1603: III.13.661).

the pandemic, some of us sought (and indeed welcomed) distraction, while simultaneously becoming more aware than ever of our mental bandwidth and capacity to attend. 'I can't focus, I struggle to read or think', writes Julia Bell (2020: 49) in *Radical Attention*, a sentiment echoed in news articles like 'I Have "Pandemic Brain". Will I Ever Be Able to Concentrate Again?' (Korducki, 2021) and studies that highlight degraded attention post-Covid-19.[12] Trade publications on distraction and our ability to attend have proliferated in the past few years, reflecting (while also deepening) the sense that we have lost our ability to focus, or, worse still, as Johann Hari suggests in his recent book, that it has been stolen from us: 'our collapsing ability to pay attention is not primarily a personal failing', he argues, but 'is being done to us all' (Hari, 2022: 9).[13] It is perhaps inevitable that readers of these books (and of the present Element) will have other things competing for their attention as they try to focus: an email swooshing in at the top right of a screen, the temptation to check the news, scroll through social media, put the kettle on. At stake here is the difference between active and passive attention, a distinction articulated by Lucy Alford in *Poetic Attention*:

> Active, or endogenous, attention is characterized by an intentional work of attention in which the subject deliberately and purposefully focuses his or her attention on the object at hand. . . . In passive, or exogenous, attention, the subject's attention is caught and held by changes or movement in the environment, or by the sheer arresting nature of the object itself. (Alford, 2020: 33–4)

Alford's model of exogenous attention strongly resembles the kinds of distraction to which this Element attends. Distraction, as it is treated in what follows, refers to a variety of attention that shifts and drifts – is

---

[12] See, for example, Sijia Zhao et al. (2022) on the persistence of attention and memory deficit after recovery from mild Covid-19.

[13] For recent trade publications on this subject, see Phillips (2019), Eyal (2019), and Bar (2022).

pulled, caught, or held – from centre to periphery, that encourages not a loss of attention but a wandering and widening of it. To paraphrase Dryden, we are sure to be better for the wandering.

Paying Attention: Attentive Audience vs Distracted Multitude

What does it mean to be attentive to performance? How is that attention paid? In 'An Excellent Actor', John Webster describes the actor in the theatre as the centre of attention: 'Sit in a full Theatre, and you will think you see so many lines drawn from the circumference of so many ears, while the *Actor* is the *Centre*' (1616: sig. M2r). The description recalls the etymological sense of attention as a kind of linear stretching, with auditors connecting directly with the actor on stage who 'charms [their] attention' (Webster, 1616: sig. M2r). Such attentiveness was, however, by no means guaranteed, and scholars have emphasised that early modern theatre was 'generally seen as a distracting and distractable environment' (Lyne, 2020: 7), where there 'prevailed a kind of dialectic between distraction and attention' (Dawson, 2001: 91). As Bruce Smith reminds us, '[y]ou can *hear* sound waves with a certain range of frequencies and a certain range of amplitudes, but you can choose to *listen* with varying degrees of attention' (1999: 6). In his recent study, William N. West emphasises the early modern interest in what took place off and around the stage, as well as on it:

> Playing drew on what was around, refiguring and replaying it: Reformation concerns with representations and communities; travel across the river; bears in Southwark; apples in mid-flight; cutpurses potentially everywhere; brawling; noise; food. These seem to have caught the consciences of early modern playgoers far more than what seem to us necessary questions of the play. (West, 2021: 5)

Replicating a 400-year-old performance space – open air, an audience almost in-the-round, roughly a third of them standing, and a lighting state that is (mostly) shared between actors and spectators – the experience of playing and playgoing at Shakespeare's Globe is at odds with the modern conventions and expectations of theatregoing. Mainstream, proscenium arch theatre is constituted by a particular kind of attention, where focus is directed towards the stage space through technologies of lighting and sound. To risk a generalisation, one might reasonably expect, in this kind of theatre space, to sit in silence in the dark while lighting pulls focus towards the stage, perhaps even towards a specific actor. That audience behaviour and attention in these spaces is bound up with issues of light has been explored by critics such as Caroline Heim, who highlight the impact of the gradual darkening of theatre auditoriums that came with the introduction of electric lighting into theatres in the 1880s, in tandem with the implementation of theatre etiquette in the mid-nineteenth century, on how audiences 'perform':

> The absence of a lit space in which to perform and to see and be seen had one of the most significant impacts on audience performance. On a practical level, as the theatre auditoriums were one by one darkened during the late nineteenth and early twentieth centuries, accounts of audience performance by audience members and actors diminish significantly. Audiences could still be heard, but were no longer seen. (Heim, 2015: 65)

With what Kirsty Sedgman terms 'the anesthetisation of audience behaviour' (2018: 25), even audience audibility might be threatened; 'what has become standard', Jean Paul Sartre notes, describing the behaviour of audiences at his *Le Diable et le Bon Dieu* (*The Devil and the Good Lord*) at the Théâtre Antoine in 1951, 'is the silence during the scenes: no coughs, no handkerchiefs. Which means that people are paying attention' (Sartre, 1976: 234).[14] The theatre auditorium goes dark, the audience falls silent. Now, pay attention.

---

[14] It is worth pointing out here that this is not a form of attention that Sartre welcomes: 'I am not too sure that I welcome this attention', he continues, 'because the audience is not at ease' (Sartre, 1976: 234). See Heim (2015: 78–9)

Pay attention. It is worth pausing over the economic implications of this commonplace phrase.[15] As Julia Bell points out:

> The verbs we use around attention are uniquely revealing. To pay attention describes a transaction, specifically a financial one. In French it is *faire attention* – make or do attention; in Spanish *prestar atención* – to loan attention. These differences somehow seem crucial to the way in which our different cultures think about time and value. In our mercantile, transactional Anglosphere, *paying* attention acknowledges a cost in everything we look at. Our attention is spent. (Bell, 2020: 51–2)

For the modern theatregoer, there is a sense that attention is not just something that one pays but also something that one pays money to experience uninterrupted. Undivided attention, considered this way, comes at a cost. There is a suggestion, Sedgman observes, 'that purchasing an experience necessarily gives that person the right to receive the experience they desire' (2018: 126). Where in London's West End the cost of a ticket typically increases with proximity to the stage, the pricing strategy of the Globe (following its early modern counterpart) inverts that model to offer the 'cheap seats' (£5) to the 600 or so 'groundlings' who stand in the yard around the stage.[16] That paying less for a ticket might impact how audiences pay attention is anecdotally mentioned by a former Globe director: 'People have more mobility', he explains, describing audience members who move around the yard, 'so they can leave ... [P]eople pay £5 often, so the sort of investment is much less' (EoSI, [1]).[17] This sense of an alternative theatre etiquette is also noted in actor

for a discussion of this as an example of restrictions on 'audience performance'.
[15] On the cost of paying attention in Shakespeare's work, see Langley (2018).
[16] At the time of publication, the cost of a ticket ranges from £5 (standing) to £62 (seated).
[17] Some EoSIs cited in this Element have been anonymised. In these instances, interviews have been numbered and corresponding Collection Level Reference numbers have been provided in the bibliography.

interviews: 'it's a very honest thing, there's none of that etiquette that you get with in-the-dark theatre', explains Graham Butler (EoSI, 2012); 'people … might not follow conventional theatre etiquette all the time, you know, I think that's great' (EoSI, [2]). As we will see in what follows, attention in this theatre is focussed, invested, paid, and paid for, somewhat differently.

*

Focussing on the reconstructed Globe on London's Bankside, this Element considers attitudes and responses to distraction in modern performance. Bringing into focus the kinds of distractions that audiences and actors respond to in the space, Section 1 gives space to diversion, drawing on show reports and actor interviews to introduce the kinds of distraction that disrupt and contribute to performance in this theatre. This archival material will, at times, impose upon and disrupt the main text, parenthetically interrupting prose and drawing attention to the periphery. In so doing, this section seeks to productively complicate attention in a way that echoes the theatrical space under consideration, formally echoing the distracted dimension of performance where the sudden downpour of rain, a pigeon landing on stage, snippets of overheard conversation, or a hovering helicopter can temporarily disrupt the action. Having briefly introduced the distractions that might impact or inform performance in the space, Section 2 attends to a phenomenon that features heavily in discussions of distraction at the Globe: fainting. Here, I offer a sustained reading of the affective potential of the distractions that occur in the peripheries and edges of performance, gesturing towards a way of accounting for and attending to the interplay between the central and the marginal. Section 3 then turns to document the Globe's response to the Covid-19 pandemic, where the dynamics of distraction – of being drawn apart – figured in socially distanced playing and playgoing. In what follows, distractions and diversions are considered not as deviations but as an integral part of the experience of performance at the new Globe.

1 Distracted Trajectories: Tracing the Detour

In the epic poem *De rerum natura* (*On the Nature of Things*), the first-century BC Epicurean philosopher Lucretius described how the random deviation or swerve of an individual atom from its path could have considerable consequences. For Lucretius, this slight and random turn brings about all events, all things; atoms fall through space in a straight line, until one unpredictably swerves – known as a *clinamen* – causing atoms to collide, combine, cluster together, and take on new forms:

> Unless inclined to swerve, all things would fall
> Right through the deep abyss like drops of rain. There would be no
> Collisions, and no atom would meet atom with a blow,
> And Nature thus could not have fashioned anything, full stop.
>   (Lucretius, 2007: II.220–3)

This is, as Jonathan Goldberg puts it, 'the originary deviation from which everything follows' (2009: 59); 'Whatever exists in the universe exists because of these random collisions of minute particles', Stephen Greenblatt (2011: 188) explains. Creation and form are products of deviation. The world is fashioned by a distracted trajectory.

Lucretius offers a philosophical model for constructive and destructive deviation, establishing the potential of the swerve, the detour. The metaphorical potential of the *clinamen* has informed theorists and writers from the Renaissance to the twentieth and twenty-first centuries – from John Donne, Margaret Cavendish, and Michel de Montaigne to Harold Bloom, Gilles Deleuze, Jacques Derrida, Michel Serres, and Virginia Woolf (to name just a few). For these writers, the swerving atom connotes the individual, free will, a narrative path, a mode of reading. The collisions occasioned by the *clinamen* are aleatory points at which relations between and among elements shift – 'bottlenecks, knots, foyers, and centers; points of fusion, condensation, and boiling; points of tears and joy, sickness and health, hope and anxiety, "sensitive" points' (Deleuze, 2015: 55).[18] There is great energic potential in these 'sensitive' points – unique moments of tension that occur within the otherwise continuous flow of events: the overflows, bends, turns, tipping points, intensifications where change occurs and where things, people, emotions come together, fuse, erupt, boil over.

---

[18] Deleuze's concept of 'singularities', described here, draws heavily on Lucretian atomism. See, for example, Johnson (2016).

As irruptions of or detours from the regular, these points and events are not reproducible: they are governed by chance, accident, digression.

The connotations of this model of creative errancy and collision, as a way of thinking about performance, will be given space to stack up and accrete in what follows. Here, the atomic swerve informs my sense of the sudden disruption of or departure from linear attention: a kind of interruption or derailment capable of causing chaos and disorder, but also of constituting a unique theatrical event. Distractions, like the swerving atom, pull things off course. Where critics such as Stephen Greenblatt (1988) and Eric Langley (2014) have used the clinamen to read the structural principles of plays like *Twelfth Night* and *The Comedy of Errors*, what follows allows atomism to inform a reading of performance at the Globe. Here, as in Shakespearean comedy, 'you reach a desired . . . destination not by pursing a straight line but by following a curved path' (Greenblatt, 1988: 71). Following the distracted trajectory of the clinamen, this section explores events and occurrences where attention swerves, pausing over the 'turning points' where it veers, shifts, and constellates in unexpected places, in order to suggest that such deviation generates theatrical meaning, energy, and pleasure. Here, I trace the detour. As Jacques Derrida has it, 'instead of tackling the question or the problem head on, directly, straightforwardly, which would doubtless be impossible, inappropriate, or illegitimate, should we proceed obliquely?' (1995: 12).

Weather

I am not a day of season,
For thou mayst see a sunshine and a hail
In me at once. But to the brightest beams
Distracted clouds give way. So stand thou forth;
The time is fair again.
(All's Well That Ends Well, V.iii.32–6)

> *The weather changed rather quickly from sun to torrential rain.*
> *Many of the [g]roundlings initially tried to brave it out,*
> *but eventually gave in and took shelter in the Foyer.*
> *Door 4 became very congested with groundlings trying to avoid*

> *getting wet and umbrellas going up. FOH asked for all umbrellas*
> *to be put away and ensured the entrances were kept clear.*
> (show report, *Julius Caesar*, 25 July 2014, matinee)

Weather in outdoor performance has the potential to inform how we attend, what we are attentive to, for how long, and how susceptible we are to distraction. In *Weathering Shakespeare*, Evelyn O'Malley points to the number of studies that 'variously demonstrate how the weather influences human behaviours, emotions, financial markets, productivity, mood, physical and mental health, emotional vulnerability, self-control, risk perception, the way media cover the news, tipping in restaurants, dating, flirting, hitchhikers' successes, aggression in sports, how we measure life satisfaction, and whether we show up to vote or respond to surveys' (2020: 18).

> *During the first act it was very crowded,*
> *hot and humid in the theatre.*
> (show report, *Antony and Cleopatra*, 22 June 2014, matinee)

The nature of an open-air playing space renders players and playgoers alike open to these affects – a particular instance of which will be discussed in Section 2 of this Element – and contributes to the variability, 'liveness', immediacy, and theatrical pleasure that the space can generate. As David Williams observes, 'all outdoor site work necessarily engages with the unpredictabilities of weather, either opening itself to the generative possibilities of weather's creative agency within the work ... or (fruitlessly) trying to deny it entry to the site as "container"/backdrop' (2006: 142). The 'mercurial weather', as Billington (2000) put it at the outset of this Element, is a key contributor to the variable performance conditions at the Globe, and a sense that the weather impacts both audience and actor attention rings throughout the actor interviews. Weather is distracting in the space in that it both detracts from the action and threatens to fragment audience cohesion. As one actor described during a particularly hot summer, 'it is so outrageously hot at the moment ... there are a lot of distracted people from that, it's very difficult at the moment to feel them as a cohesive whole that you can use' (EoSI, [3]).

Beyond its obvious implications for the playgoer standing uncovered in the yard, rain in particular impacts the experience of playing at the Globe: 'the acoustics change in the theatre [after it has rained] . . . you have to be aware of the acoustics, that they do change because of the weather' (EoSI, [4]). Changes in weather bear on the space's soundscape, dampening or enriching sound depending on the conditions.[19] A key issue that punctuates actor interviews, however, is the distractions that come with 'bad' weather: 'Strangely enough, what I find is the biggest distraction are those bloomin' coats they sell when it rains, because the noise of the rain hitting those plastic coats is much louder, and much more distracting that any helicopter. . . . If a lot of people buy them it'll drive you to distraction because it's constant then' (EoSI, [5]). The 'fantastic noise generated by rain on plastic', Jonathan Cullen notes, is 'like a sort of white noise', meaning that 'you do have to put up your vocal energy quite a deal' in response (Cullen, EoSI, 2011). 'There is', another actor describes, 'a sort of rustle of macs and chats about it starting to rain . . . [T]hey sort of forget that you are acting. I saw *Henry IV* the other day and it started raining in Part One and I sort of did the same' (EoSI, [6]); 'when it is absolutely pouring down you are dealing with people with their macs on . . . and it's just impossible to be heard' (EoSI, [7]).

Torrential rain fell from 14.28 with several
lightning strikes within close proximity.
(show report, *Antony and Cleopatra*,
22 May 2014, matinee)

Very, very wet, causing the yard to
empty steadily throughout the show.
(show report, *Antony and Cleopatra*,
27 May 2014, evening)

Bad weather, and responses to it, distract from and disrupt the action, and occasion a change in playing and playgoing, a switching of gears in response.

[19] On weather and acoustic geography, see Blesser and Salter (2009: 338).

But there is also a sense that particularly bad (wet) weather, as well as being a distraction that can fragment an audience – distinguishing seated spectators who have the shelter of a roof from the groundlings who do not and might subsequently leave the theatre – has the capacity to unify audiences; 'The weather changed them [the audience], and that was interesting', notes director Jonathan Munby: 'How they are unified by inclement weather' (Munby, EoSI, 2008). Where O'Malley (2020: 10) signals a 'temporary fellowship' between audience and actor that is produced by laughter at references to rain when there is none, some actors point to the connection that is unlocked by virtue of experiencing weather together:

> one of the great romances of the Globe is that it forces the groundlings especially to have a real connection and affinity with you that they are getting wet, you are getting wet and yet you are continuing playing. . . . It is a shared experience so they share the rain. If you share the rain with them they will enjoy it. (Joseph Marcell, EoSI, 2011)

With the fragmentation of distraction comes the opportunity for fellowship, unity, and cohesion. While fleetingly treated in isolation here, weather will continue to inform readings of distraction in the discussions that follow.

Seeing the Audience

There are distractions that get seen that otherwise wouldn't at other theatres.
. . . It's sort of nice to catch people's eyes and smile, you know. . . .
We live in a very digital age and the live experience is still something.
(Gary Shelford, EoSI, 2015)

'Technological and material factors', Evelyn Tribble (2011: 37) explains in her study of cognition in Shakespeare's theatre, are 'essential in understanding attention. Contemporary theatres rely heavily upon the technology of lighting to literally throw focus on particular stage areas and to attract the audience's eyes.' Lacking this technology and instead replicating the original 'shared' lighting conditions of its early modern counterpart, the reconstructed Globe uses light to widen rather than direct audience attention.

> *One person talking to a friend this afternoon really quite*
> *powerfully takes attention away from the stage.* (EoSI, [8])

In the first scholarly monograph on this theatre, Pauline Kiernan explored the implications of the theatre's shared lighting state: 'the absence of stage lighting and design to direct and control the audience's attention require[s] the actors to work harder to draw the audience into the fictitious world' (1999: 6) .

You can see if they're yawning. You have to fight for the audience's attention.
(Sean Holmes, quoted in SGT, 'Findings from the 1995 Globe Workshop Season Report', 1995)

In the open-air Globe, actors and audiences share the same light: for evening performances, where natural light fades, artificial lighting is used to light stage and audience spaces alike. The theatre therefore makes available and encourages a multi-directional gaze: as well as seeing actors on stage, audience members can see one another, observe one another's reactions, distract and be distracted, and in turn pull focus from the stage action.

It's a bit like watching a tennis match because their heads flip
from one side of the stage . . .

> *. . . to the other depending on who's talking.*
> *So you start speaking and it feels almost like a wind as 700 heads*
> *turn and look at you and then when you stop speaking the whole lot*

look the opposite way and that ... is not something I've
experienced before. (Matthew Flynn, EoSI, 2012)

Furthermore, actors can see their audiences, creating what Barbara Freedman describes as a kind of 'fractured reciprocity, whereby beholder and beheld reverse position in a way that renders a steady position of spectatorship impossible' (1991: 1). 'You can feel attention and you feel lack of attention, but it's more visible, you can't cut away from it here' (EoSI, [9]): a shared lighting state means not only that attention is less fixed and directed than in a proscenium arch theatre but also that shifts in and absences of attention are rendered visible, sometimes disruptively so. 'If something's going on', one actor describes, 'you see the audience shift, just out of curiosity like "what's going on over there?"': 'what throws me', they continue, 'is that huge shift to whatever the distraction is' (EoSI, [10]). 'The fact [that] you can see the audience is sometimes distracting', Michelle Terry agrees (Terry, EoSI, 2015); 'it's tricky, and you can sometimes see in the audience that they're not engaged – it's tough ... it's so easy to be distracted' (EoSI, [11]).

As well as being able to observe audience engagement, or lack thereof, the shared lighting in the space also renders visible the unusual mobility of the Globe's playgoers.

People aren't afraid to chat, fidget, move around which
is part of the joy of what this theatre does but it's
sometimes difficult to deal with. (EoSI, [12])

Just as attention wanders in this theatre, so too do audiences: 'I see people distracted and people leaving', one director explains; 'it's quite hard to watch people leaving your own show' (EoSI, [1]). Show reports from the 2021 season frequently note the mobility of the audience, observing, for example, 'lots of movement in and out of the theatre throughout the performance' (show report, *A Midsummer Night's Dream*,

25 August 2021, evening) and 'lots of patrons moving about the yard' (show report, *Romeo and Juliet*, 7 September 2021). These dynamics of distraction – indeed, it is here that its etymological sense of being pulled away or drawn asunder is, literally, spatially played out – are often described as a key part of the Globe experience, for better or for worse:

It's lovely to see people wandering
around the yard . . . I always did
that as an audience member.
(EoSI, [13])

    People coming in and out,
    especially if you've got a tender
    moment, is difficult, but it's just
    something you learn to accept.
    (EoSI, [14])

        [I]n this theatre you can see people
        milling around . . . and changing
        position and it sort of energises the
        play a little bit like it wouldn't do
        elsewhere. Normally that would be
        a distraction but here it sort of helps.
        (EoSI, [15])

Hot weather, feeling faint, the desire to get a better or different view, long run times, or lack of interval (as was the case in 2021, discussed in more detail later) all variously present themselves as phenomena that provoke audience movement and disrupt stasis, such that can signal both engagement and its absence. This kind of literal, physical distraction is, in other words, part of how an audience member might attend. Certain productions are particularly 'moving', not necessarily in an emotional sense (although that may be the case), but in their determination to move audience members around the space; *Titus Andronicus* (2006, 2014), for example, dis-

> *Our carts demand the audience to shift, as in medieval times.*
> *They also echo the processional parades of classical Rome.*
> (Lucy Bailey, *Titus Andronicus* programme interview, 2006)

-tracted groundlings by repeatedly wheeling actors through the yard on carts and towers, or by carving out room for the pit scene by unfurling a net to create a pocket in the space of the standing spectators. While distraction was here used to engage and involve audiences, some actors have suggested a correlation between stillness and focus: that a more concentrated (that is, more densely populated) yard contributes to audience concentration. 'The more packed the yard is, the less people move ... so everybody's a lot more still, more focussed', suggests one actor (EoSI, [16]). This reading of audience concentration features elsewhere in interviews: 'I think when the theatre's very full, the focus is very tight, without you having to do much. ... Things really focus. Everybody is compelled to look, somehow, people move about less because they have less space, maybe because they are seen they feel more exposed so they don't move as much' (EoSI, [17]). 'You could feel the focus', the actor continues. There is a phenomenology and tangibility of attention here, bound up with (and perhaps derived from) the experience of seeing the audience and of the audience themselves being seen: both by actors and by one another. Attention and distraction, as we will continue to see in what follows, are not only rendered visible in this space but also physicalised, embodied, felt.

While the theatre aims to preserve the shared lighting state through the evening, as mentioned, there is inevitably a difference between matinee and evening performances as natural light is gradually replaced by the artificial. 'It is well known and easy to retrace in literature that some days, and mainly some parts of the day, are very atmospheric', writes Tonino Griffero (2017: 108). Although the audience is partially lit in evening shows, actors observe a shift in the atmosphere, and in the quality of audience attention, from day to night. Jolyon Coy, for example, suggests that 'the attention seems to be more focussed in an evening performance, and a little bit more

dispersed in a matinee' (Coy, EoSI, 2014), while another actor similarly felt that 'in the evening [the space] is more like a normal theatre.
I think the contract with the audience really diminishes' (EoSI, [17]).
The capacity for light to alter a performer's contract with the Globe
audience was perhaps debated most intensely following the use of
amplified sound and artificial lighting under the artistic directorship
of Emma Rice (2016–18): a debate that would ultimately lead to her
departure after just two years in post.[20] It was an issue that deeply
divided both the Globe and its audiences, exposing fault-lines between
'innovative/traditional,   museum/theatre,   conformist/experimental,
accessible/elite, commercial/artistic, amplified/acoustic, artificial/nat-
ural' (Dustagheer, 2021: 65). At stake here was a sense of modern
technology as a 'distracting interference' that drew and pulled the
organisation away from 'a more direct interaction with, a more com-
plete immersion in, the "spirit" of Shakespearean drama' (Worthen,
2017: 420). At stake, too, was the direct interaction with the audience:
while performers had previously noted diminishing levels of audience
visibility from matinee to evening and midnight matinee performances,
actors during the 2016 and 2017 seasons experienced these variable
lighting conditions in, for want of a better phrase, a more amplified
way. When asked about how seeing the audience informed or changed
her performance in the space – as was routinely asked across the EoSI
programme – Kirsty Bushell, who played Juliet in Daniel Kramer's
2017 production, drew a key distinction between matinee and evening
shows. Unable to see audience members through the lights in the
latter, Bushell described the former as feeling more 'honest': 'I just
imagine them there ... you've got something that is a bit dishonest if
you like, whereas in the daytime it's completely honest: I'm talking to
them, they can see I'm talking to them and I think maybe the ...
afternoon shows do tend to be a bit more emotional, for the
audience. ... Although they don't get the amazing lights that we

---

[20] On the Globe, Emma Rice, and technology, see Worthen (2017).

have' (Bushell, EoSI, 2017).[21] As well as describing a slightly different contract with the audience by virtue of the lighting state, Bushell also observed a shift in her own focus as a performer:

> with lighting on you, you can obviously see the director really pinpoint [things] ... it's something about being wider ... but under the lights you have to be more focused – not more focused, but a different kind of focus. Definitely when I was all under the lights, I found myself sharpening beats up ... you are literally being seen under a different lens, so I guess it is as if it was on telly or something like that, you just shift. (Bushell, EoSI, 2017)

For actor and audience alike, performance under lights directs focus, sharpens beats, whereas shared light involves 'being wider', stretching performance technique and widening the lens of attention.

'Vehicles of Attention': Sensing Distraction

A very noisy afternoon with helicopters,
church bells and multiple activities on site.
(show report, *Romeo and Juliet*, 22 August 2021, matinee)

The Globe requires actors to compete with, respond to, or incorporate the distracting phenomena that prompt audience attention to momentarily shift, to swerve away, to detour through. From the chimes of the St Paul's church

---

[21] Reflecting on their performance during the season immediately after Rice's departure, when the theatre was transitioning back to shared lighting, one ensemble company member similarly used the term 'honest' to describe playing in shared light, commenting that evening shows had become easier to play than matinees owing to the fact that only a small portion of the audience was visible to them: 'you don't have the distractions', they noted, admitting that they had found themselves 'playing more with the groundlings, which is a problem because that directs your attention downwards rather than up and out' (EoSI, [3]).

bells across the river to the sound of musicians on the Southbank, the noisy party-boats journeying down the Thames to the smell of incense or food on the piazza, the theatre's open-air design allows for external sounds and smells to be carried into the space. For audiences, as we have seen, the Globe's shared lighting state means that the field of vision is widened beyond the actors on stage to include fellow audience members, architectural features, the open-air sky, all of which have the potential to disrupt, pull, and stretch attention in different directions. Sensory experience in the space renders attention mobile, tractable; as Teresa Brennan describes, the senses are 'vehicles of attention' (2004: 136).

> *Towards the end of the first act and immediately after the*
> *interval the theatre was subject to significant overhead air traffic.*
> (show report, *Antony and Cleopatra*, 27 July 2014, matinee)

Overwhelmingly in the EoSIs, the most common response to issues of distraction in the Globe is the noise of planes and helicopters. The theatre is positioned under a flightpath, meaning that planes and helicopters frequently fly over during performances. Often unable to compete with a noise, an actor must decide whether to acknowledge the offending aircraft, pause

A helicopter circled the Globe at 20.10 . . .

speaking, and 'wait it out', thereby pausing (and therefore

. . . Another helicopter flew along the Thames at 20.35.
(show report, *Julius Caesar*, 2 July 2014, evening)

fragmenting) the action, or try to speak over it. 'Helicopters are worse because they stay longer', one actor explains (EoSI, [18]): 'you can't compete with them at all', noted another (EoSI, [19]). Concerns surrounding disruption from aircraft include the fact that it 'can take people out of the world' (Jack Monaghan, EoSI, 2015), or that it 'ruins a punchline' (Michael Bertenshaw, EoSI, 2011). Acoustic distraction, in particular, frustrates and fractures action.

Several patrons left due to the noise of the helicopter.
At points it was very difficult to hear. Some patrons
at the end were asking for refunds.
(show report, *A Midsummer Night's Dream*, 31 August 2021, matinee)

As well as threatening to disrupt action and speech, the kinds of background noise that are occasioned by the open-air space have broader implications for how different audiences attend; given that not all audience members experience and respond to sensory data in the same way, responses to distractions in the space vary. Background noise may pose challenges to audience members who require a hearing aid loop, for example, while, as Sedgman notes, 'the sensory differences of autistic people may make the absence of all distractions an essential requirement for concentration' (2018: 100). This applies to performers as much as it does to audience members. One actor, for example, who experiences hyperacusis or noise sensitivity, described performing against certain sounds and frequencies – for example babies crying – as a particular challenge of performance in the space, which amplifies and bounces certain sounds around: 'my focus is really split and I'm quite anxious about where the sound's coming from, when the sound's going to happen and then modifying my reaction to it so I can stay in the scene' (EoSI, [26]).

And then you hear the bells of St Paul's across the river
... And it just reminds you there's a world outside of the theatre,
and it's ... bigger than you. (EoSI, [26])

Modifying or adjusting performance in response to distractions at the Globe is not always straightforward, and, like the disruptive sound-scape, the tractability of attention that the space invites, coupled with its poor sightlines, can also pose challenges to performances that require visibility. In Michelle Terry's inaugural season as artistic director in 2018, Nadia Nadarajah joined the ensemble cast as Guildenstern in *Hamlet* and Celia in *As You Like It*; as a Deaf actor, Nadarajah used British Sign Language (BSL), which was also adopted by some members of the company in shared scenes. Gemma Miller's review of *As You Like It* highlighted that the use of BSL on stage required a new kind of attention from both actor and audience: 'It was a bold choice,' writes Miller (2019: 71), 'not only because it required the other actors to sign their lines when she was on stage, but because it demanded close attention from the audience, not an easy task in a theatre with restricted sightlines and multiple distractions'. In her EoSI, Nadarajah explained that while she was not herself distracted by the sound of aircraft, allowing for these shifts in attention nonetheless informed her performance in the space and on-stage interactions with the company:

> I know hearing people get really annoyed by helicopters. They don't bother me. Fortunately they [the actors] give me a clue, like they'll subtly say helicopter, they'll just place that sign, and then I understand why people have stopped. At first I was like 'why has everyone stopped? What's going on?', and then they told me subtly. . . . I can't hear it coming, I just see it overhead and . . . you've all got that audio cue that it's coming. (Nadarajah, EoSI, 2018)

For productions that incorporate signing, distractions that draw the eye away from the actors on stage, coupled with the near-in-the-round design of the space, can be inherently problematic: loss of visual

Pigeons!
A pigeon came up on stage the other day and
started eating the Doritos in the middle of the
balcony scene. It was great.
(Golda Rosheuvel, EoSI, 2017)

attention risks missing signs, and therefore missing dialogue. The wider attentional focus that shared light offers can mean that sign language necessarily competes with the distractions in the space; 'for me lighting is essential', Nadarajah explained: 'I need to be seen. . . . I thought that in a matinee performance it would be easier to see me, but actually it turned out that in the second [evening] performances it was easier to be seen because we were lit as well. We weren't just having to rely on sunlight' (Nadarajah, EoSI, 2018). Adjusting for the different lighting states between matinee and evening also required that careful attention be paid to costume, which needed to contrast Nadarajah's skin-tone to ensure visibility, but also be plain so as not to 'strobe out' signs, something that was similarly at risk in instances where audience visibility was disrupted by direct sunlight.

Turning to the experience of the playgoer, UK theatres such as the Globe and the Royal Shakespeare Company (RSC) have introduced 'relaxed' performances (known as 'sensory-friendly' performances in the USA), which, as Sonya Freeman Loftis (2021: 55) notes, 'include changes to lighting and sound (to decrease sensory overload), reduced ticket sales (to cut back on crowding), and additional support to prepare audiences for the show'. Taking the recent production of *Twelfth Night* (2021) as an example, the Globe also offered familiarisation tours of the theatre, as well as a 'Visual Story' (Shakespeare's Globe, '*Twelfth Night*: Visual Story', 2021) which included a 'Sonic Story' (Figure 1) – created by disabled-led company Touretteshero and commissioned by the theatre – that illustrated the rough timing, intensity, and source of various sounds that could be heard during the production.[22] Charting the acoustics of the space, this snapshot captures and maps a theatrical soundscape that feels quite particular to the Globe: music, singing, audience response, voices of actors moving through the yard, the bells of Saint Paul's marking the hour from across the river.

A distracting space, the theatre continues to explore ways in which it can enable all audiences to attend. For some audience members, those elements of the Globe space that might be considered distracting – shared light, audience mobility – make it easier to attend; 'not only does performing outdoors under natural light automatically reduce some of the autistic sensory sensitivities introduced by many modern theatre spaces', Loftis (2021: 55) highlights, 'but a relaxed attitude towards theatre etiquette during regular performances can also go a long way to welcoming neurodiverse audience members'. In these circumstances, a less sharp, wide-angled attentional focus facilitated by shared light, coupled with the distracting elements of performance explored earlier, can make the space more accessible – a model of the distracted Globe, indeed of theatre more broadly, that

---

[22] For more information about Sonic Stories, see William Renel (2019).

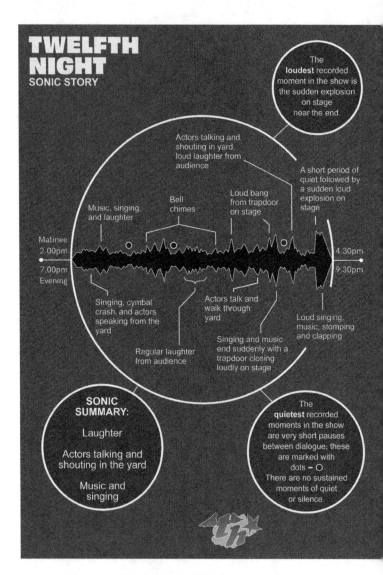

Figure 1 *Sonic Story of Shakespeare's Globe's 2021 production of* Twelfth Night.
Source: Touretteshero CIC, 2021.

can be attended by all perhaps involves not the mitigation of distraction but rather an accommodating of and creating space for it.

Happy Accidents

> *Those moments . . . they're real. . . . It's not television or film.*
> *We're there. We're doing it, together. . . . That's the beauty I*
> *think of this space particularly . . . because anything can*
> *happen and you have to be open to that.*
> (Golda Rosheuvel, EoSI, 2017)

'It is useful', writes Sara Ahmed (2010: 22), 'to note that the etymology of happiness relates precisely to the question of contingency: it is from the Middle English word *hap* suggesting chance.' Happiness, she continues, 'puts us into intimate contact with things' (23): happiness not only is about chance (i.e. the happenstance) but also signals a coming together (i.e. haptic, from the Greek ἁπτικός or *haptikos*, to come in contact with). While the distractions mentioned here have generally tended to signal a coming apart, I want to pause over moments where they have the opposite effect: where a chance occurrence happily coincides with performance, where things fall together.

In his discussion of the form of the essay and its digressive tendencies, Theodor Adorno describes a model of 'unity' that can be gained 'only by moving through the fissures, rather than by smoothing them over':

> The essay must let the totality light up in one of its chosen
> or haphazard features but without asserting that the whole
> is present. It corrects the isolated and accidental aspects of
> its insights by allowing them to multiply, conform, and
> restrict themselves – whether in the essay's proper pro-
> gress or in its mosaic-like relation to other essays; and it
> does so not by abstracting characteristic features from its
> insights. (Adorno, 1984: 164)

Here the haphazard and the accidental are not figured as hindrances to a unified whole but rather as productive, necessary, constitutive features that ought to be allowed and given space: fissures do not irreparably fragment the whole, but are part of the journey towards coherence.

> *Everyone just comes together for that one moment*
> *going, that was really special and it wasn't planned*
> *and, yeah, it's amazing.* (Imogen Doel, EoSI, 2016)

In performance, such journeying from disparity to unity might be figured in terms of the spectator who becomes, or is felt to become, part of 'the audience': 'After two and a half hours . . . the show has turned a disparate bunch of individuals into one collective mass laughing and applauding at the same thing[;] it sort of tunes everyone in together' (EoSI, [20]). In some cases, distraction is figured as something that threatens such cohesion: 'if you have 1500 people you bring them together into a single unit. If people start heckling or messing about or fainting . . . then it splits it up into 500 different units, and you have to draw them all back together again' (EoSI, [21]). There is also, however, a sense of the 'haphazard' and 'accidental aspects' of performance, distractions that might threaten to disrupt or derail it, as having the same unifying potential that Adorno describes. 'I think audiences like it when something happens to disrupt a show, and in those moments, everyone is engaged with the same moment if you acknowledge it' (EoSI, [22]). Often in the interviews, distractions at the Globe are, paradoxically, described as an effective way of bringing an audience together. 'What I have seen . . . is that for the moments that you lose them, the fact that everyone carries on, including the audience, means that there's almost a turn-up in volume of concentration afterwards. So for the moments that you've lost it they come back to you with more eagerness, so you are sort of rewarded for the distractions', Janie Dee explains (Dee, EoSI, 2011). Here, to borrow Michel Serres' description of atomic errancy, 'order comes stochastically from disorder' (2018: 113).

*[O]f course it's irritating when a helicopter sits over the top and hovers for hours . . .
but it also makes for something different, and the amount of times when you get a
happy accident, where something happens out of the ordinary that gives you a pay
off, that also can't happen in other theatres. . . . I think the Globe has a little bit
of magic . . . because you are only there that night and the show you're watching will
only happen this night and the things that occur can only happen in this environment
in this way at this point.* (James Garnon, EoSI, 2011)

Describing the unique playing conditions at the Globe, Garnon highlights the formative potential of the happenstance, the chance occurrences and coincidences that the open-air space occasions. Accounts of 'happy accidents' particularly constellate around weather and birds. 'There are times when a bit of happenstance occurs', notes one actor (EoSI, [23]), describing an interaction with a black bird during the banquet scene in *Macbeth*. 'There was a black bird that landed on me once at our feast, at the second feast with Banquo, when I say . . .

> Augurs and understood relations have
> By maggot-pies and choughs and rooks brought forth
> The secret'st man of blood. (III.iv.126–8)

. . . and there was a fucking black bird on stage!' Elsewhere, one *As You Like It* (2009) company member similarly recalled the 'coincidence or serendipity' of a pigeon landing on stage, only to be shooed away by Dominic Rowan (playing Touchstone): 'and then his very next line was "as pigeon's bill, so wedlock will be nibbling" . . . It's a great way of bringing the audience even closer, saying this is happening to all of us' (EoSI, [24]).

*I think actually these days I really love distractions
you know. . . . You don't have to do hardly anything,
it's just acknowledging what is happening, for the
audience to derive huge pleasure. . . . I guess because*

you're suddenly in this sort of shared moment
together, and they like it more I would say than
anything else. (Helen Schlesinger, EoSI, 2019)

Thus the happenstance unites actor and audience: theatrical form and pleasure come from chance.

Elsewhere, a pigeon figures as a reincarnated Antony in *Antony and Cleopatra* (Sirine Saba, EoSI, 2014), a helicopter coincides with a reference to 'Venus' pigeons' in the 2014 production of *The Merchant of Venice* (EoSI, [25]), gloomy weather means that the 'atmosphere' became 'really Scottish and grey and sort of made the evil' in *Macbeth* (EoSI, [23]). More recently, Sophie Russell, who played Malvolio in the 2021 production of *Twelfth Night*, described the Globe atmosphere through a description of a similar chance encounter that coincided with the performance:

> There was one point when I was being Malvolio where I was doing the speech (I don't know what speech it was, probably in the letter scene where there's a lot of speeches). I had a pause in the speech and this crow came and flew on to the thatch and cawed, and he looked exactly like he was my spirit animal because he was a crow (and Malvolio's like a crow [n.b. Malvolio in this production had a black quiff]). And the whole audience kind of looked, and I noticed him and he spoke his line at exactly the right time, like he was going 'yes, Malvolio', and the whole audience felt the same. I could feel it – they all channelled that into the crow. And then it came and sort of fluttered down for a bit, and then fluttered away. But the timing of the crow and the scene and the character was beautiful. He never came back. Crows come down, but they don't speak at the same time, every night. It's those moments where magic happens, that can only have happened because you've got the sky and the

world. And there's loads of those. And that's a good distraction. (personal interview, 21 December 2021)

Common to these kinds of descriptions is a sense that happy accidents
can bring about theatrical pleasure and meaning. In the Lucretian model
of atomic inclination, atoms are taken off course and stack together to
generate new forms and events. At the Globe, the distracting conditions
listed here all have the potential to derail a performance, to induce
chaos, as grains of attention are detracted from the action on stage. But
responses to issues of distraction overwhelmingly signal that the chance
event, the atomic swerve of attention to something beyond the stage,
can positively constitute performance in the space, and that the best
performances, those that really come to life, are those that allow for the
detour, that recognise distraction to be simply part of the nature of
things.

2 Attending to Distraction: Feeling Faint

The most interesting word, if we give it back its Greek . . . is *to pathos* =
what one feels, as opposed to what one does, and also as opposed to *hè
pathè*: passive state. . . . I don't believe I am forcing the word; in
philosophy: *ta pathè* → the events, the changes that occur in things →
to pathos: shimmering field of the body, insofar as it changes, goes
through changes. (Roland Barthes, 2005: 73)

In *The Neutral*, Roland Barthes (2005: 101) offers and encourages an
encyclopaedia of affects, calling for 'a hyperconsciousness of the affective
minimum, of the microscopic fragment of emotion . . . which implies an
extreme changeability of affective moments, a rapid modification, into
shimmer'. 'The kind of "psychology" we need', he argues, '. . . is an
inventory of shimmers, of nuances, of states, of changes (*pathè*)':
a '"patho-logy"' (77). Observing the 'changes that occur in things' and
in bodies, this section considers the patho-logy of distraction in the Globe

through sustained attention to the 2014 revival of *Titus Andronicus* (dir. Lucy Bailey, first performed in 2006). Here, I explore the 'ripple affects' of distraction, and how specific distractions register on and between bodies. In so doing, I consider how it feels to be distracted in this particular space, and how such feelings (both physiological and emotional) are encouraged, fostered, and shared.

Pulling Focus

The Globe, as we have seen, is a theatrical space where it is easy to pull focus, and for focus to be pulled. Actors in the space describe how easily audience attention can be drawn; 'the slightest thing takes their attention', notes Michael Bertenshaw: 'if you respond too much ... the slightest gesture, you see all the eyes go like that [mimes shifting view]' (Bertenshaw, EoSI, 2011). For directors working in the theatre, the distracting phenomena listed in the previous section, along with the fixed, static design of the space, generate an anxiety about the theatre having the power to 'pull focus' from the productions that take place within it. 'The aesthetic of the building is problematic from my point of view', Jonathan Munby notes, as he directed *A Midsummer Night's Dream* in 2008:

> Our job is story-telling and to hold the attention of 1500 people ... anything that inhibits the control of the audiences, I think, shoots us in the foot and makes our work harder. Those factors are many and varied. ... Performing against the colour and decoration of the façade is a major factor. It feels like the actor, and the voice, are in competition with the decoration. Once we made the decision to hide the decoration and colour, with an all black plain façade, it controlled the image and allowed the voices to be heard. The resultant clarity was astonishing. (Munby, EoSI, 2008)

The design of the space, for Munby, raised issues not only of attention but also, when coupled with the kinds of distraction identified in the previous section, of tension: 'Can you ever create tension in that space – I mean truly? There are so many factors that will disrupt that moment. 500 people on their feet constantly moving. Noise pollution ... Can you ever really create that tension?' (Munby, EoSI, 2008). What sits behind Munby's questions here is a concern that the theatre might better lend itself to, is more accommodating of, comedies rather than tragedies; if, as Matthew Bevis (2017: 173) signals, 'attention is a form of "tension"', the distracted Globe threatens to shatter it.

That distractions have more utility for the comic actor than performers in tragedies emerges from interviews with actors who have worked in the space, where there is a sense of distraction as a gift for comic actors which is often felt to be unavailable to or challenging for tragic scenes. 'I think birds and rain and things you can bring into your performance, but only if you're a comic character could you acknowledge the planes', noted one *Henry VIII* company member (EoSI, [9]). Charles Edwards describes something similar: 'Acknowledging those things [rain, helicopters, 'accidental moments'] within the performance can only really happen either in a soliloquy or in a comic sequence or in a lighter sequence. I think trying to do that would obviously destroy – trying to do that in a serious or emotional scene would be a mistake' (Edwards, EoSI, 2011). Noting the distraction of people leaving the theatre, Bertenshaw also theorised the potential for genre to impact response: 'if you are playing a comedy part it does not bother you but if you are playing a serious part it probably does' (Bertenshaw, EoSI, 2011). A tragedy, former artistic director Dominic Dromgoole hints in his discussion of *King Lear*, requires more focus: 'you're not able, as you are with a comedy, to tickle them [audiences] and open them up, you require a certain amount of attention' (Dromgoole, EoSI, 2008).

Directing *Timon of Athens* in the 2008 season, Bailey shared Munby's sense of the threat to focus posed by the space: 'Jonathan's absolutely right, I think – there's so much distraction. That's why we put roofs on and nets on and try, working very hard, to get people to watch the action and listen to the actor, without wandering off' (Bailey, EoSI, 2008). To create 'a more concentrated space', one must first eliminate unwanted distractions. Approaching *Titus Andronicus* in 2006 and 2014, theatrical 'tension' would similarly rest on the creation of an atmosphere that focussed attention, rather than allowing it to wander too freely.

Something in the Air: Attending to Atmosphere

'Is there anyone who has not, at least once, walked into a room and "felt the atmosphere"?' (Brennan, 2004: 1). Recent literature on affect has begun to explore how atmospheres radiate and circulate through spaces, with critics of New Aesthetics such as Gernot Böhme defining atmosphere as a 'spatially extended quality of feeling', an ecstatic intertwining among things, persons, and environments: 'they are affective powers of feeling, spatial carriers of mood' (2017: 20). For Böhme in particular, a consideration of atmospheres through 'the ecstasy of things' marks an interest less in how 'things' might be thought of as distinct from other 'things' and rather in the way in which 'things' step out of themselves (21). Key here is the affective potential that things emanate; 'atmospheres', he suggests, are 'not thought of as free floating but, on the contrary, as something emanating from and produced by those things, people or their constellations' (Böhme, 2017: 23). In this, Böhme's thinking seems to align with that of Tonino Griffero, who considers 'atmospheric empathy' as a kind of 'corporeal tuning between object and perceiver' (2014: 134). Subjects, spaces, and objects, these theorists stress, can become 'tuned', tinged with emotion or mood that in turn affects their atmosphere and vice versa.

From sound effects and incense, to actors moving audience members around the yard, to William Dudley's design, Lucy Bailey's *Titus* created an intensely sensory atmosphere that was variously described as 'edgy', 'stifling', one that 'sets one on edge immediately' (Hemming, 2014; Kirwan, 2014; Orman, 2014). The Globe is known for its elaborately painted scenic façade, (faux) marble pillars, and open-air playing, but this production plunged the theatre into darkness, wrapping the stage and pillars in black cloth and covering the 'roof' with velarium – an awning used in Roman amphitheatres to protect spectators from the sun – that enabled Bailey and Dudley 'to create chiaroscuro – to control the sunlight and create light and shadow' (Lucy Bailey, 'Re: Titus', email to the author, 18 September 2022). The production's design, very simply, not only flattened the distracting elements of the space but smothered them; as Farah Karim-Cooper observed: 'It seemed, at first, as though the entire auditorium was living under threat, oppression, a new kind of occupation' (2008: 67). In her review, Lyn Gardner (2014) described how 'Bailey's production – which has the incense whiff of the charnel house – wraps the action around the audience so that the groundlings become the citizens of Rome'; it is 'as if the entire world has been plunged into mourning'. As Bailey clarified in an email, 'we were trying to create a temple of death' (Bailey, 'Re: Titus'). The space, these responses suggest, was 'tuned' with feelings of mourning and claustrophobia, facilitating a kind of atmospheric empathy that 'tuned' audiences in turn. This stifling, claustrophobic, edgy atmosphere was one that Bailey and Dudley had actively sought to create:

> The challenge of the Globe is how to create atmosphere, without the use of theatre lights and amplified sound. The velarium created light and shade, it trapped the incense and the smoke. Smell and smoke literally hung in the air. By wrapping the stage and pillars, Christo-like, in black cloth, the actor's bodies and faces were seen in relief and had much more presence. (Bailey, 'Re: Titus', 2022)

The relationship between bodies and space was crucial to the creation of this production's atmosphere; bodies in this space not only were 'tuned' but were themselves part of the tuning. As well as experiencing the production's atmosphere, audiences also contributed to it. Akin to Böhme's description of atmospheres as 'moving emotional powers, spatial carriers of moods', the Globe audience became part of that emotional movement: carriers of it, entwined in it.

Responding to the affective, cognitive, and bodily turns in critical and theoretical thinking, modern Shakespeare scholarship has begun to rethink audience experience in the early modern and present-day theatre. Most recently, Stephanie Shirilan (2021) has emphasised the ways that the early modern body extended into its affective surroundings through attending to experiences of shared breathing and immersive pneumatic experience, positing a model of 'respiratory sympathy' that highlights the risks and rewards of breathing together and the communities that such an experience creates. In this model, feeling is understood as something that can be communicated atmospherically, carried on the air, breathed in and out. The affective relationship among atmosphere, air, and feeling was particularly significant for Bailey in *Titus*. '[S]moke like incense doth perfume the sky' (*Titus Andronicus*, I.i.148): the 'incense whiff of the charnel house' that Gardner described above was one of the ways that the production 'wrapped' around its audience, that the production's atmosphere became felt and immediate. As affect theorist Teresa Brennan (2004: 9) highlights, smell is 'critical in how we "feel the atmosphere"'. According to Bailey, incense was used 'to get the smell and taste of death into the space, to make it pungent'; 'I wanted to make things physical and visceral', she clarified: 'plus the incense – well, there we had our strange, heady slaughter space' (Tripney, 2015; Woodall, 2016). A useful example of the kind of 'entrainment' that scholars have identified in the Globe space – a kind of radical connectivity where individuals fall into synchrony, 'lock into each other's rhythms of . . . movement, speech and gesture' (Shaughnessy, 2015: 27) as well as posture and breathing – smell here 'tuned' and primed audiences for the kind of tragic response the production would ultimately elicit. Just as Holly Dugan (2014: 209) has argued of the early modern playhouse, the smelling of 'vapors' at the modern Globe may be considered a 'critical component and effect [and affect] of performance'.

Ripple Affects: Distraction and/as Emotional Resonance

'Laughter is contagious at the Globe', explains Amy Kenny (2015: 42) in her study of this phenomenon in the space. In part, she suggests, this is 'because people can see others laughing right next to them. . . . Laughter moves through the theatre like a ripple effect, or a wave at a football game, spreading and gathering momentum from the audience itself' (42). Unlike black-box theatres where the audience faces forwards in a dark space, the Globe's (almost) in-the-round shape, combined with its universal lighting state, 'incites laughter far more than in other theatrical spaces' (Kenny, 2015: 42). Considered in these terms, the space has a distinct affective energy and capacity, one that allows 'for a more comedic atmosphere for the audience'; far from being passive onlookers, the Globe audience, in this model, contributes directly 'to the humour found in plays', and in turn to a performance's creation of meaning (Kenny, 2015: 48). The tragic potential of Kenny's comic model – where emotional response is understood as a product of architecture, atmosphere, and emotion that ripples around the theatre – was fully exploited by Bailey's *Titus*, which made UK headlines as a 'gore-fest' that 'takes out 100 audience members' (Clark, 2014). Although somewhat misleading ('100' being a cumulative number at that point in the run rather than the number of fainters during any particular performance), this headline draws attention to another phenomenon that is common in this theatre space; as critics such as Penelope Woods (2016: 1542) have highlighted, fainting has become 'a notable feature of the current Globe audience'. There are a number of in-house theories for why people faint in this theatre-space, including issues of ventilation and air circulation, hot temperatures, the slight incline of the floor in the yard, and the impeded circulation of blood of spectators standing for long periods of time. Fainting, then, was not entirely unique to the production of *Titus* – show reports, particularly in high summer, indicate that it is common to have one or two patrons fainting, feeling faint, or falling ill during a performance.[23] But the high number of patrons

---

[23] For a recent exploration of audience illness in the Globe FOH reports, see especially Tribble (2022).

who fainted during the run of this particular production suggests that there may be more in play here.

The Globe's FOH show reports record details of each individual performance, including run time, audience size, weather, and first aid notes. Documenting *Titus*' run from 25 April to 13 July 2014, the reports feature what critics including Rob Conkie (2021), Stephen Purcell (2018), and Penelope Woods (2012) have identified as an 'ongoing fainting narrative' (Conkie, 2021: 33).[24] Details of audience members who leave feeling faint or unwell, and those who are escorted from the theatre in wheelchairs after fainting, punctuate these reports: 'Between 20.45 and 20.59 there was a succession of ten patrons feeling unwell and exiting. All were treated for symptoms of fainting and sickness. One girl collapsed in the yard and was taken out by wheelchair. One lady collapsed having left door two on the Piazza. Five of these patrons left for home' (show report, *Titus Andronicus*, 24 May 2014, evening). The show report from 2 May, for example, gestures towards the frequency of such incidents in its observation that this was a 'very quiet show from a first aid perspective'. Often, the reports make an effort to distinguish between patrons who fainted and those who left the theatre feeling faint, ill, or due to the weather, and at times the member of staff writing the report offers up explanations for particularly high faint counts: 'we had a lot of patrons faint throughout the show, due to the weather, as well as the content' (show report, *Titus Andronicus*, 7 June 2014, evening). Weather in particular does seem to be a contributing factor to symptoms of fainting and dizziness; the faint count is often at its highest when the weather is described as 'hot and humid', sometimes as 'hot and dry'.

As common explanations as to why people faint at the Globe, however, weather and temperature only go so far. A comparative look (see Table 1) across three productions of Shakespearean tragedies that ran simultaneously during the summer of 2014 offers an example of where this sense (both in-house and in the media) of *Titus* as a stand-out production in terms of its faint count emerges:

[24] While Woods' study pre-dates this production, it offers valuable observations about fainting patrons in an earlier (2006) run of the production, as well as in Lucy Bailey's *Macbeth* (2010).

Table 1 *Cumulative number of patrons recorded to have fainted in the Globe 2014 show reports.*[25]

Titus Andronicus	Antony and Cleopatra	Julius Caesar
241	83	129
across 49 shows	across 57 shows	across 51 shows

One pattern in the data on fainting during shows of *Titus* is the time that it occurs: overwhelmingly, and perhaps unsurprisingly to those familiar with the play, instances of fainting occurred in the first half of the show, just before the interval, in the scene where Lavinia emerged mutilated and covered in stage blood (Act 2, Scene 3). Reviewer Holly Williams, who herself fainted during the performance, put her experience down to the quality of performance: 'A confession: I fainted. I'm not alone: audiences are dropping like flies at this revival of Lucy Bailey's infamously gory 2006 staging. . . . The swooning is testament to Flora Spencer-Longhurst's astonishing performance as the raped and butchered Lavinia' (Williams, 2014). Here, 'Spencer-Longhurst jerks and twitches like a wired, traumatised doll', 'totter[ing] about, quaking' (Gardner, 2014). There is, perhaps, a physical synchrony or entrainment between actor and spectator in play here, a shared rhythm whereby one kind of radical bodily response (twitching, jerking, quaking) has the capacity to affect another (fainting). As Amy Cook (2011: 259) points out in her discussion of cognitive and embodied interplay, an audience might leave a theatre 'imitating voices or the

[25] These figures represent the number of patrons who were reported to have completely fainted in the show reports for each production. Table 1 does not include patrons who were reported to have left the theatre 'feeling faint' or 'unwell' – I have included tables with these data in the Appendix (Tables A1–A3). It is worth noting here that fainting occurred across a wide-spectrum of theatregoers: there does not appear to be any particular age or gender bias. The majority of patrons who fainted were situated in the yard (i.e. standing), but there are also a number of instances of fainting in the upper and middle galleries (seated). Performances where FOH reports were not available have not been included in Table 1. Also not included are FOH reports for performances that took place in the Sam Wanamaker as part of the 2014 'Outside In' experiment.

bodies of those they have seen onstage; after two hours of simulating the actions and feelings performed onstage, perhaps there is a level at which spectators and performers come together'. What comes into focus is a kind of emotional resonance between actor and spectator that manifested itself in the physical experience of fainting: a vibration of feeling experienced both emotionally and physically.[26]

The emotional and physical feelings of audiences of *Titus Andronicus* have been studied by the RSC. Joining up with market research company Ipsos MORI in 2017, the theatre conducted a research project that monitored the emotional engagement (via heart rate) of three different types of audience of their production (dir. Blanche McIntyre): a live theatre audience, a cinema audience who watched the production via live-stream, and a group who viewed it through a 360-degree filmed virtual reality (VR) experience on VR headsets.[27] The study, Pippa Bailey (Head of Innovation at Ipsos MORI) noted in a press release issued by the RSC on 26 October 2017 (RSC, 'Press Release: Shakespeare Still Has Power to Shock'), allowed for an understanding of 'how people respond, what they attend to and how they react'. In all, 107 participants took part in the study, with results suggesting that levels of positivity, engagement, and shock were higher among the live theatre audience, 'with more attention to the elements of staging, costume, set, plot, music and choreography' (RSC, 'Press Release', 2017). The attentional lens of the theatregoer appears to have been wider. Cinema audiences, by contrast, appear to have had the lowest level of emotional engagement, and lower 'shock levels'. That said, the RSC also reported that the cinema audience found the production more

---

[26] On emotional resonance and contagion, see especially McConachie (2008), pp. 65–120.

[27] According to the RSC press release on 26 October 2017, the VR experience was created by Gorilla In The Room, and was played through HTC VIVE VR headsets. While theatre and cinema audiences watched the performance in two halves, the VR participants watched the production in five parts, including two five-minute breaks in each half in addition to the normal interval. The filming took place from the position of someone in the front row in the auditorium, with participants able to experience a full 360-degree view of the theatre.

'moving' than their theatre and VR counterparts, which the press release theorised as being 'possibly due to the cinematic style directing the viewer's eye to the details of actor expressions (e.g. [a] tear rolling down Lavinia's cheek) which are often missed by theatre audiences' (RSC, 'Press Release', 2017). How and to what one attends, the study suggests, have clear implications not only for issues of theatrical engagement but also for how theatre makes audiences feel.

To return to the Globe, what is perhaps most striking about the 2014 show reports for *Titus Andronicus* (from which I quote in this paragraph) is the frequency with which they describe patrons who fainted in 'quick succession' or near simultaneously: 'Tonight again there was a quick succession of fainters from 20.45–20.55' (1 May, evening); 'Tonight again there was a quick succession of fainters from 20.35–20.55. Three people went down in the yard one after the other, three more went down ten minutes later followed by one in the upper gallery' (4 May, evening); 'we had a quick succession of four fainters' (11 May, evening); '8 people fainted in the yard between 20.30 and the interval [20.58]' (22 May, evening); 'succession of ten patrons feeling unwell and exiting, all [of whom] were treated for symptoms of fainting and sickness' (24 May, evening); 'between 15.15 and 15.30 six patrons fainted inside the theatre' (29 May, matinee); 'we had twelve people out feeling overwhelmed, nausea[ted], and light[-]headed. Six people fainted in the yard during this time' (8 June, evening); 'An hour into the first half, FOH had twelve nearly simultaneous faints across all Lower Gallery doors' (5 July, midnight matinee). While the phenomenon of multiple patrons feeling faint or fainting at the same time is recorded with particular frequency during the run of this production, it is not exclusive to it: other shows in the 2014 season, for example, record similar instances of patrons fainting around the same time as one another.[28] More recently, a show report specifically reports a 'sympathetic fainter' who

---

[28] The show report for *Julius Caesar* on 31 July 2014 (matinee) notes: 'we had four patrons faint in quick succession, one from the middle gallery, the others from the lower gallery'. A report for *Antony and Cleopatra* on 7 August 2014 (evening) describes 'two patrons who fainted from Door 3 in the first half in quick succession, both in their twenties, one male, one female'.

fainted at the same time as another patron during *Romeo and Juliet* (23 September 2021, evening). At stake here is a form of emotional resonance not simply between actors and spectators – where audiences feel pathologically attuned to a character's suffering and experience in turn a kind of physical suffering themselves – but between spectators themselves; the distraction of one theatregoer can distract another. In a space where audience members can see each other, and where emotions are acknowledged as spreading and rippling through audiences, there is scope to consider the kind of negative, more violent effects that the kind of corporeal tuning outlined earlier can have on spectators' bodies and minds.

That fainting contributed to the atmosphere marks *Titus* out from other Globe productions. Discussing *As You Like It* (2015), Gary Shelford explained the impact that distractions like fainting can have on performance:

> There is a chance that it can break the atmosphere. If someone faints like they did the day before yesterday it does ... you know, [be]cause you start thinking ... 'Are they ok?' But you still gotta keep talking and you can see, you know, a lady being helped away by ushers and you're aware that the rest of the audience can see that. So there are distractions that get seen that otherwise wouldn't at other theatres. (Shelford, EoSI, 2015)

This is not to suggest that actors in *Titus* were not concerned by the high number of fainters during the run: 'I'd hate to say it's something we're proud of, or anything', explained Matthew Needham, 'We're not[;] I find it, it's upsetting. [But] it means that the show's doing something ... ' (Needham, EoSI, 2014). In *Titus*, the phenomenon of fainting contributed to and became part of the atmosphere, rather than being something that threatened to break it. 'In a very dark way', explained Jake Mann, 'it's great that it's been affecting people to that level that they feel so involved with it that it causes them to pass out' (Mann, EoSI, 2014). While it may be impossible to tell how far audiences felt 'involved' in the production, attention to the production's 'deliberate creation of an atmosphere', to borrow Brennan's (2004: 16) phrase, suggests its capacity to 'envolve' – entangle, enfold – them.

The distracting potential of the production drew in audience members keen to see it in action (the best thing is perhaps to suggest that the reader take a quick detour here and run search terms like 'Titus droppers' and 'Titus fainters' through Twitter). Curiously, where the show reports might allow us to consider fainting as a kind of radical 'sympathy' – a symptom of the Globe's unique performance conditions, of the violence of the drama, of the kind of shared patho-logy that the space makes possible – such responses, by contrast, can seem markedly unsympathetic. 'People fainted? Lol, pathetic': so reads one comment under a review that references the production's high faint count; 'Oh come on', reads another: 'it's fiction not real life for goodness sake!' (quoted in Burrows, 2020: 102). Here, then, is sympathy both in excess and in absentia. Taken in combination, such responses raise questions about the pathological potential of performance more broadly: how can feeling be shared when feeling is performed, and not authentic? How can we know how audiences feel, and how can we measure that felt experience? Marina Warner's review offers one answer: 'What we are feeling as we sit there in the Globe – what perhaps the "droppers" are experiencing – is recognition, the ancient principle of storytelling' (Warner, 2014). The moment of recognition (or *anagnorisis*), as I have been suggesting throughout this Element, does not sit wholly within the drama but ripples out beyond it, encompassing and drawing on the distracting events and phenomena at the periphery, in ways that critics are only just beginning to explore and theorise. What attending to these kinds of distraction offers is a recognition (that is, both an acknowledgement and a rethinking) not only of 'what we are feeling when we sit there in the Globe', or what the '"droppers" are experiencing', but of how we feel it, and how those feelings occur, register, and resonate in this theatrical space.

3 Our Distracted Globe: Playing in a Pandemic

'Alone, Together'

Nature has certainly touched all of our lives in recent months. Whilst everything seems so uncertain, one thing we know for sure is that the world will never be the same again. In 1599, when Hamlet stood on

a 'distracted Globe' and uttered the words: Now I am alone – he would
have been surrounded by up to 3,000 people. Now we are alone, but we
are also in the company of billions, from all around the globe, finding the
most inspiring ways to be alone, together. In these times of isolation, we
will continue to reach people on our 'distracted Globe', providing community, joy, and wonder, remaining, albeit digitally for now, a place of
connection for us all. (Michelle Terry, quoted in Shakespeare's Globe,
'Press Release: Globe Announces New Digital Content', 30 March 2020)

In March 2020, the Covid-19 pandemic closed London's theatres. Like
theatres across the world, the Globe moved its activities online, streaming
past performances and pre-show talks to virtual audiences. Here, as the
pandemic distractedly fractured the globe, Hamlet's lines acquired new
meaning and resonance. Moving online, the Globe launched a 'Love in
Isolation' series – or rather relaunched the Guardian's 'Shakespeare Solo'
series – where actors and members of the public performed speeches from
their place of self-isolation, and streamed six previous productions for free
on YouTube, starting with *Hamlet* (2018) on 6 April 2020, and followed
by *Romeo and Juliet* (2009) on 20 April, *The Two Noble Kinsmen* (2018) on
4 May, *The Winter's Tale* (2018) on 18 May, *The Merry Wives of Windsor*
(2019) on 1 June, and *A Midsummer Night's Dream* (2013) on 15 June. Each
production 'ran' for two weeks, accumulating 2.7 million views and
increasing the Globe's YouTube subscribers by 729 per cent
(Shakespeare's Globe, 'Shakespeare's Globe in Lockdown: One Year
Later', blog, 18 March 2021). On 11 May, the theatre also streamed its
2020 Playing Shakespeare with Deutsche Bank production of *Macbeth*,
and made available thirty-four short videos that had been commissioned
as part of the 2012 Globe to Globe Festival. Responding to the distracted
present, the globe/Globe sought alternative ways for audiences to be
'alone, together'.

   Hamlet figured centrally in the theatre's response to the pandemic. It
was, as noted above, the first production that the theatre launched for time-
limited release in April 2020, bringing in a virtual audience of 600,000 across
its 2-week run. As Pascale Aebischer observes in *Viral Shakespeare*, *Hamlet*

was the Shakespeare play 'that appeared in the greatest variety of versions' across a number of theatres, including puppet, avant-garde, and operatic adaptions alongside three German versions and more mainstream performances (Aebischer, 2021: 40). Reflecting concerns about isolation, mortality, and contagion, *Hamlet* seemed to speak to the current moment, and theatres turned to Shakespeare's most distracted play in order to reach and connect with audiences in the most distracted of times. In turn, this shift to digital performance brought with it a kind of distracted spectatorship; one could be part of an audience while being physically separate from other spectators, watching or listening to a play while also doing other things like cooking or communicating with others during online 'watch parties', virtually together while isolating at home.

Streaming productions was not a new phenomenon in April 2020, but it necessarily became theatre's dominant mode of transmission. The kind of attention that is (or is not) paid to online broadcasts is, as Erin Sullivan has noted, markedly different from the 'focused, undivided attention from audiences' that had 'long been the default ideal' when it came 'to meaningful theatrical experience'; as a result, Sullivan continues, 'some people have objected to the idea of streamed theatre on the grounds that it is easier to get side-tracked while watching it' (Sullivan, 2020: 105).[29] Where that ideal was already disrupted for the Globe spectator, as we have seen, there is perhaps a sense in which audience attention to a streamed production might be more focussed. No longer one's own director of photography, the way an audience member attends to a production in a pre-recorded or live-streamed format necessarily means that focus is more linear and directed, with the peripheral (helicopters, birds, fainting spectators, stewards, weather) remaining just so.

With the explosion of material during lockdown also came a new form of distracted attention; with digital theatregoing, an intensified sense of time out of joint. 'The temporal dislocations of a lockdown', Peter Kirwan and Erin Sullivan observed, 'have complicated the idea of co-presence and the normal passage of time. Past productions are present; present productions disappear after limited periods;

---

[29] See also Sullivan (2022).

a production remains available while the experience of watching it at a moment of crisis passes; memories of earlier viewing blur with a fresh visit' (Kirwan and Sullivan, 2020: 491). Describing the experience of binge-watching multiple versions of *Hamlet*, Aebischer highlighted implications of this sudden concentration of these productions on one's concentration: 'the concentration of versions distracts the viewer from the thing they are watching at that moment as their mind wanders through the various versions, seeing new connections as the versions bleed into and contaminate one another' (2021: 25) . Here, then, is a kind of distraction that pulls attention away from the production at hand and towards 'new connections', simultaneously fragmenting and pulling one's sense of a text together as it is observed through different frames, different productions: a kind of unity through the fissures.

That *Hamlet* in particular spoke to the current moment was further signalled by the Globe's 'Thoughts of the Week' blog series, where artistic director Michelle Terry reflected on recent events through Shakespearean quotations that 'relate to, and express, the mood of this uncertain time'. Across a series of seventeen posts between 4 April and 14 August 2020, *Hamlet* was the most frequent play to be cited, featuring three times. Firstly, discussing the power and fragility of the mind in the early stages of the pandemic, Terry cited Hamlet's sentiment that 'There is nothing either good or bad, but thinking makes it so', describing the distraction of keeping busy as a form of emotional well-being (Shakespeare's Globe, 'Thought of the Week: The Power of the Mind', blog, 17 April 2020). Later, on 29 May (Shakespeare's Globe, 'Thought of the Week: The Readiness Is All', blog, 2020), Terry paused over Hamlet's 'readiness is all' speech – 'There is special providence in the fall of a sparrow. If it be, 'tis not to come; if it be not to come, it will be now; if it be not now, yet it will come; the readiness is all' (*Hamlet*, V. ii.191–4) – meditating on the immediate issues of mortality and the 'undiscovered country' of life after death.

On 13 June, the 'Thought of the Week' turned to Hamlet's 'Remember thee!' speech, responding to the recent murder of George Floyd, and the removal of the Edward Colston statue during a Black Lives Matter protest in Bristol. 'Our beautifully distracted globe is in the most memorable of times, in which questions about who we are, and who we will become, have never felt more urgent or more vital', it began: 'As a statue of Edward Colston is removed in Bristol, as the devastatingly disproportionate number of people from black, [A]sian and minority ethnic groups continue to die from Covid-19, as yet another light is shone on systemic injustice, racial intolerance, and institutional inequities, as history repeats itself once more, it's hard not to ask: how did we get here?' (Shakespeare's Globe, 'Thought of the Week: Remember Thee!', blog, 2020).

Where Hamlet's original reference to the 'distracted globe' might have positioned the theatre as a medium of memory, 'as a place where memories, for example of the nation's past, can be recollected in performance' (Karremann, 2015: 123), it now signalled a tension among history, memory, and the distracted present, a moment of radical pause that directed the gaze simultaneously backward and forward:

> Remember thee!
>
> Will this time pass and lessons go unlearned? Will this time pass and nothing change? Will we remember this moment with pride or regret?
>
> In our 'distracted globe', will we remember this time at all? (Shakespeare's Globe, 'Thought of the Week: Remember Thee!', blog, 13 June 2020)

Attending in a Distracted Globe

When the Globe reopened on 19 May 2021, its former 1,600 capacity was reduced by three-quarters to around 400. Audiences were socially distanced and the yard, a space formerly occupied by 600 standing 'groundlings', held only 40. For the first time, these 'standing' seats were seated, configured around the stage individually and in pairs (see Figure 2).

As restrictions gradually lifted throughout the summer, the theatre transitioned slowly back to its normal capacity. When *Twelfth Night* opened on 29 July, the Globe offered 200 standing tickets 'for those who choose to

Figure 2 *Patrons seated in the yard and sitting in socially distanced bays at the Globe for the* Midsummer Night's Dream *open dress rehearsal, 18 May 2021.*

Source: *Photograph by Pete Le May.*

social distance in the Yard', which would 'incrementally increase throughout the summer until the end of August when 400 Groundling tickets will be available for each performance'. In a 19 July press release, the theatre also outlined plans to return to full capacity:

> Seating capacity will also gradually increase throughout the summer with spaces between groups sat on the same row remaining until mid-August. The open-air theatre has laid out plans to be back to full seated capacity by 23 August. The maximum capacity of the Globe is normally 1,600 and the theatre will return to full Groundling capacity (circa 600–700) at a future date. Since May, The

Globe has welcomed over 32,000 audience members into 79 performances in our open-air theatre. (Shakespeare's Globe, 'Press Release: Shakespeare's Globe Announces the Return of Standing Tickets', 2021)

Performances during the season ran straight through without an interval, averaging just under two hours and fifteen minutes in length.[30] 'There is an imperative to keep it short, and there is a certain point in both those plays [*Twelfth Night* and *A Midsummer Night's Dream*] where there's ... an attention lull', explained Sophie Russell, who performed in both productions (personal interview, 21 December 2021). But she also noted the advantages to this model: 'no interval is great for us – the story goes on, you don't have to stop' (personal interview). Speaking to *The Guardian*, Michelle Terry echoed this sentiment: 'Terry said there is a momentum and accumulation in Shakespeare's plays which is best not disrupted. An interval breaks "a tension that he is deliberately trying to create"' (Brown, 2021). Intervals, in these terms, might be considered the ultimate distraction: an enforced break that fragments the action into two halves, breaking the atmosphere for a fifteen-minute return to reality before attention returns again to the drama.[31] This is not to suggest that audiences were to remain fixed in their seats for the show's duration: distractions historically common to the Globe such as people leaving or wandering around were not things of the past, but were highlighted as being occurrences accommodated both by the plays and by the space. 'The joy', notes Terry, 'is you're not fixed in your seat. If you need to get up and go to the toilet you can, if you need to get up and get a breath of fresh air, you can go, because we also know that he [Shakespeare] said everything at least three or four times. If he really wants you to know something he'll make sure he repeats it' (quoted in

---

[30] Based on the Globe's approximate run times as listed online: *Romeo and Juliet* (1 hour 50 minutes), *A Midsummer Night's Dream* (2 hours 20 minutes), *Twelfth Night* (2 hours 30 minutes).

[31] One ensemble company member noted the difficulty of managing audience attention after an interval: 'they [audience members] are very distracted after the interval and they're very hard to pull back in' (EoSI, [3]).

Brown, 2021).[32] 'Shakespeare doesn't mind if you're not concentrating on the play all the time', as Terry put it to me: 'the structure of the play is able to cope with that fragmentation, I think' (personal interview, 18 March 2021). In a time of distraction, the Globe, like the plays, could accommodate, even encourage, the detour.

'The Readiness Is All'

'The readiness is all and Shakespeare's Globe is ready' (Shakespeare's Globe, 'Announcing Summer 2021 at the Globe', blog, 2021). As the Globe prepared to open its doors at the end of the second wave of the pandemic in late spring 2021, I spoke with Michelle Terry about the way Covid-19 was altering and informing rehearsal practices. Before the pandemic, Terry had adopted an 'open door' policy for rehearsal, with staff members across the organisation encouraged to come and go as they pleased, just as the theatre audiences do (Figure 3).

During the 2018 and 2019 seasons, Terry had sought to create 'a kind of shortcut to the distraction when we couldn't rehearse in the [main theatre] space' by seeking to 'create distraction in the room':

> You're doing it for a space you can't possibly pre-empt; no matter how much directors wish they certainly could control it, you really can't. So the open door gesture was really a means to start dismantling that from the off. Someone will walk in and out of the yard . . . A tour will come in while you're rehearsing. It's nothing personal. (personal interview, 18 March 2021)

Returning to the Globe in early 2021, however, signalled a shift in the 'distracted Globe' ethos: 'The rehearsals, rightly and understandably, will be fragmented, will be staggered,' Terry explained, 'so there's that awful

---

[32] Some audience members seem to have struggled with the lack of interval, however; a number of show reports note 'complaints about lack of interval' (show report, *A Midsummer Night's Dream*, 20 October 2021, evening), with 'lots of customers commenting that the show was too long . . . With quite a few visitors leaving before it had finished' (show report, *Twelfth Night*, 10 August 2021, evening).

Figure 3 *A sign on the door to the rehearsal room of the Globe Ensemble (2018).*

thing where you may not see someone, in the play that you're in, until you get into tech rehearsals' (personal interview). Now the companies faced new challenges and disruptions; companies were to rehearse outside or in smaller groups, would remain socially distanced, and would slowly aim to get 'match-fit' for performance – 'vocally fit, physically fit, emotionally fit' (personal interview). To return once more to the etymological sense of distraction as a drawing asunder, a forcible disruption or division (OED, n.1a), the pandemic distracted the experience and running of the theatre like never before.

It is here that we see the spatiality of distraction most keenly, as social distancing measures necessitated division, severance, dispersion. For creatives and members of FOH in the 2021 season, becoming 'match-fit' involved a thorough risk-assessment of all safety measures in line with government guidance. As well as regular (twice-weekly) Covid-19 testing, the 'Principles

Figure 4 *Actors in socially distanced rehearsals for* A Midsummer Night's Dream, *Shakespeare's Globe, 2021.*

Source: *Photograph by Tristram Kenton.*

of COVID safe rehearsing/performing' (hereafter 'Principles') at the Globe stated that 'all creatives including performers should be 2 m apart at all times' (with the exception of 'fleeting movement' [3 seconds maximum] past one another), and 'wear face coverings (masks not shields)' which could be removed when 'rehearsing a scene or performing'. These rules also held on stage (see Figure 4): all shows were created with the 2 m distance rule in place, with any movement through the yard being subject to risk assessment so as to reduce contact with the audience, and as a continuous run (i.e. with no interval) in an effort to 'limit audience gatherings' ('Principles'). In terms that were familiar to us all during this time of uncertainty, the document ends with the note that 'all of the above guidance is subject to change at short notice'.

In practice, making a show Covid-19 compliant involved detailing and rethinking all activities where actors might come into contact or share props with one another. 'How do you get the idea of someone touching without actually touching? And keeping two metres apart?': Tour Director Brendan O'Hea articulated a key challenge of performance during this time, where the absence of touch necessitated new creative approaches (O'Hea, 'Meet the Director – Globe on Tour', 2021). In the touring production of *As You Like It*, therefore, the wrestling scene became a choreographed fight with bamboo, while the wooing scene between Rosalind and Orlando brought them within, but crucially held them just out of, touching distance. For *Romeo and Juliet* Director Ola Ince, the challenges of social distancing similarly manifested themselves in scenes of passion and violence:

> The moments I struggled with[,] though[, are] Romeo and Juliet meeting and kissing at the party, and Romeo and Juliet's love scene, where it's been a little bit more difficult to socially distance. Initially I also thought the violence was going to be really hard to socially distance, but that's become quite a fun challenge. . . . Because we've had to think of ways we could fight in a modern setting that allow for two metres, . . . it's less about punching each other and more about guns and dragging each other and chasing each other with long machetes. (Ince, 'Meet the Director – *Romeo and Juliet*', 2021)

Having been 'alone, together' for the duration of the pandemic, theatre practitioners now negotiated these dynamics on the stage, finding alternate ways to perform proximity, immediacy, contact, all at a safe distance.

The first production to negotiate this new mode of distracted – fractured, separated, disrupted – theatre-making was Sean Holmes' *Dream*, a revival of the theatre's 2019 (and at the time its most recent) production. Reshaping the show necessarily involved rethinking it at a granular level, from choreography and costume to props and blocking:

Activity: Quince handing out 4x cast scripts and 1x giant script to audience
Risk: virus could be transmitted by touching surfaces, close contact.
Control measure: Moments of being within 2 m of other persons

limited to 3s fleeting contact and always to be more than 1 m from nose to nose.[33]

Activity: Lion Costume Conga

Risk: virus could be transmitted by touching surfaces. Contained area, aerosol linger, close contact.

Control measure: Lion costume to be made longer to accommodate people at 2 m intervals. Sequence to be kept as short as possible to help with aerosol lingering.

Activity: Titania Touches Bottoms [sic] recorder after it has been played
Risk: virus could be transmitted by touching surfaces/saliva.

Control measure: Not sure we can make this moment safe ... The recorder is in the mouth and blown into. ('A Midsummer Night's Dream 2021 – Covid Specific RA')[34]

Reworking this production in light of government guidelines and restrictions also had implications for the production's casting. For each show during the 2019 run, the role of Starveling was allocated to an audience member at random. Selected by a member of the cast shortly before the show went up, Starveling would be escorted to the stage via a central ramp in the yard, before being handed a large script and joining the mechanicals for the remainder of their rehearsal scenes and ultimately powering their performance at the wedding in Act 5 by a peddle-bike positioned on stage. This moment was of particular importance to Holmes: 'obviously we can't bring them on stage quite the way we did before. . . . that will be really interesting in a Covid compliant way, but we are still determined to do it because that delicate and important bond between audience and action and actors and theatre is something, as Prime [Isaac, Assistant Director] said, everyone has been missing' (Holmes, 'Meet the Director – *A Midsummer Night's Dream*', 2021). With the audience member who would play Starveling for each show unable to join the company on stage in

---

[33] The script for Starveling, handed to an audience member as discussed further on, was also to be 'newly photocopied on each occasion', following hand hygiene precautions, and disposed of at the end of each performance ('A Midsummer Night's Dream 2021 – Covid Specific RA').

[34] These extracts are taken from a table and have been reformatted here.

2021, the production came to manifest spatially the liminal position of this particular role that was at once both audience member and mechanical, positioning the character on a small, slightly raised platform just below the stage at the front of the yard (marked by a star, visible in Figure 2; the platform is also just visible in Figure 4). It was from here that Starveling would 'power' the performance of Act 5 via an exercise bike, as the character had done from a position on the stage in 2019. 'Myself the man i'th' moon do seem to be' (*A Midsummer Night's Dream*, V.i.236): somewhat aptly for a character who creates theatrical pleasure by disrupting the fiction of the play-within-the-play – calling attention to his position both within and outside the drama – this production's Starveling embodied the theatre's period of disrupted playgoing. Synecdochic in many ways of the marginal elements that this study has explored as contributing to and shaping Globe performance more broadly, the distracting potential of the pandemic meant that the driving force behind the mechanical's play – what powered it – came from the periphery.

Coda

As we emerge from the pandemic, the way that audiences attend, and attend to, Shakespeare and early modern performance continues to develop with advances in digital and immersive technologies.[35] The place for and the value of distraction in this new era remain unclear; at the time of writing, when theatres are *almost* back to some form of 'new normal', conversations about what it means to be part of an audience continue to call (demand?) us to pay attention in a certain way: since lockdown, according to one article, 'a small but noticeable percentage of audience members have forgotten how to behave in public' (Johns, 2022); in another, it seems musicians want us 'to pay closer attention at gigs' (Snapes, 2022). The overriding message here seems to be that we need to 're-learn' how to pay attention, to pay it better, to be less distracted, and less distracting.

---

[35] On Shakespeare and early modern performance in the pandemic, see Aebischer and Nicholas (2020), Aebischer (2021), Lennox and Mason (2022) and Allred, Broadribb, and Sullivan (2022).

From the outset, this Element has sought to complicate this sense of distraction as a failure or loss of attention, and to signal instead how it could more properly be considered an element of Shakespeare performance that both deserves our attention and in some sense constitutes it. Thinking about how such attention is paid, and to what, has been crucial to this endeavour. Throughout this study, space has been afforded, both literally and figuratively, to the marginal – to the events and phenomena that occur beyond the edges of the stage, but also to the archival material that sits in the peripheries of performance research. It is my hope that the constellations of material used here – performance reviews, show reports, prompt books, actor interviews, director's notes, blogs, risk assessments – illuminate the potential of the periphery to contribute to performance research, particularly in spaces and productions that so often draw energy from beyond the limits of the stage. Of particular interest for me here has been the intersections between performance and issues of affect, emotion, and embodiment, and how a close consideration of the kind of distractions that manifest in theatrical spaces like the Globe can reveal those elements to be less an obstruction to playing and playgoing, and rather an integral part of how a performance generates theatrical meaning, energy, pleasure, and 'liveness'. In making room for a consideration of distraction, we might better understand, better attend to, the experience of playing and playgoing in these spaces.

A quick call to attention. This Element offers only a snapshot of the potential of archival materials to contribute to studies of Shakespeare performance. The Globe's EoSIs in particular have as yet received little scholarly attention, and there remains much to consider with regard to how the responses of actors and creatives working in the space have shifted, for example, over time, under different artistic directorships, pre- and post-pandemic. While fragments of FOH show reports have been integrated into the above, the narratives and patterns that sit within them concerning things such as weather, audience response, and the shaping of institutional narratives and identities also present themselves as particularly fertile areas for future research. As Barbara Hodgdon (2006: 137) notes of archives, 'this stuff remains mute until someone uses it, turns it into narrative'. Finally, to direct the reader towards a call that the present Element has taken to heart, I would like to reiterate Bridget Escolme's (2010: 90) exhortation that 'where full archives exist, use all their elements in dialog'. The way that various archival elements and fragments speak to one another when placed in dialogue could have contributed countless productive detours to the present study – I hope others find them equally distracting and therefore worthy of their attention.

As I have sought to bring into focus, then, distraction is not simply something 'you have to put up with' at the Globe, as Billington (2000) had it at the outset of this Element; it is a part and product of the fabric of the space, part of how the space invites us to attend. It is, to borrow Worthen's (2003) phrase, what shapes and gives force to Globe performativity, as distractions call attention to its liminal position as both a modern theatre and a restoration of early modern theatrical experience. Indeed, to trace distractions through the archive is to see how this crucial element of performance in the space figures as a kind of memory. *Remember thee?* 'It reminds me a little bit of what the audience perhaps would have been like then' (EoSI, [19]); 'Four hundred years of a difference, and there's a constant' (EoSI, [5]).[36] If the Globe itself is a medium of memory, then distraction necessarily holds a seat.

---

[36] References to distraction as a kind of authenticity or echo of early modern theatre can be found throughout the actor EoSIs, such as Wynter (2008), Edwards (2011), Butler (2012) and Needham (2014).

Appendix
Fainting, Feeling Faint, and Illness among Audiences in the Globe's 2014 Summer Season

Below are some initial findings from the show report data on fainting, feeling faint, or being taken ill in three productions in the 2014 summer season at Shakespeare's Globe: *Titus Andronicus*, *Antony and Cleopatra*, and *Julius Caesar* (Tables A1–A3). See also Table 1, in Section 2, 'Ripple Affects', which details the number of patrons reported to have fainted in these productions. As is noted there (see n. 28), show reports for performances that took place in the Sam Wanamaker as part of the 'Outside In' experiment have not been included. Reports lacking numerical data have also been omitted, and in those where a rough number is given (i.e. 'upwards of 20 patrons'), the specified number has been taken.

Table A1 *Cumulative number of patrons reported in show reports to have felt faint, been treated for fainting symptoms, or experienced dizziness.*

Titus Andronicus	Antony and Cleopatra	Julius Caesar
172	116	263
across 49 shows	across 57 shows	across 51 shows

Table A2 *Cumulative number of patrons reported in show reports to have been taken to the first-aid room, including those feeling 'unwell' or 'sick'.*

Titus Andronicus	Antony and Cleopatra	Julius Caesar
168	74	57
across 49 shows	across 57 shows	across 51 shows

Table A3 *Combined total number of patrons reported in show reports to have experienced all of the above (fainting, feeling faint/dizzy/light-headed/sick/unwell).*

Titus Andronicus	Antony and Cleopatra	Julius Caesar
581	273	449
across 49 shows	across 57 shows	across 51 shows

*

Source: *Analyses of data on illness were conducted and written up by Jonathan P. Green, and are included here with his permission.*

Statistical models were developed to explore the factors contributing to illness among audience members at performances of three plays at Shakespeare's Globe, London, in the summer of 2014: *Antony and Cleopatra*, *Julius Caesar* and *Titus Andronicus*. The analyses included only matinee or evening performances (not midnight matinees) where audience sizes, air temperature (scored as "warm or hot" or not) and the numbers of audience members who fell ill (fainted, felt faint or otherwise felt unwell) were recorded in show reports. In total, data from fifty-two performances of *Antony and Cleopatra*, forty-eight performances of *Julius Caesar*, and forty performances of *Titus Andronicus* were included in the analyses.

Analysis

A pair of generalised linear models was used to model the proportion of audience members (i) falling ill (fainting, feeling faint, or otherwise feeling unwell) and (ii) fainting. In both cases, a quasibinomial distribution was used to account for overdispersion. Models included the following explanatory variables: play (*Antony and Cleopatra*, *Julius Caesar*, or *Titus Andronicus*), performance time (matinee or evening), temperature (warm/hot or not) and audience size. Further, P values and associated F values for each explanatory variable were obtained by comparing the global model containing all explanatory variables to a reduced model that omitted the variable of interest. Where a significant difference was detected among the three plays, post hoc Tukey tests were performed to determine which pairwise differences were significant. Tests were two-tailed and statistical significance was determined as $P < 0.05$.

Results

(i) Reports of Audience Illness (Fainting, Exhibiting Fainting Symptoms, or Otherwise Unwell)

The proportion of audience members experiencing illness differed across the three productions ($F_{2,132} = 20.00$, $P < 0.0001$). Reports of illness were significantly higher in performances of *Titus Andronicus* than *Julius Caesar* ($P = 0.0005$) or *Antony and Cleopatra* ($P < 0.0001$). Reports of illness were also significantly higher in *Julius Caesar* than in *Antony and Cleopatra* ($P = 0.04$). When controlling for the influence of other variables, the analysis revealed that audience members were more than twice as likely to fall ill during *Titus Andronicus* as in either of the other two plays.

In addition to differences in illness among the three plays, the analysis showed that more audience members fell ill during matinee performances than during evening performances ($F_{1,132} = 6.76$, $P = 0.01$). Significantly more illness occurred on warm/hot days ($F_{1,132} = 21.73$, $P < 0.0001$), but there was no significant relationship between audience size and the proportion of audience members falling ill ($F_{1,132} = 2.58$, $P = 0.11$). It is important to note, however, that the effects of temperature and audience size are to an extent confounded, since larger audiences were reported on warm/hot days ($F_{1,140} = 6.86$, $P = 0.01$). While it is clear that temperature has a strong effect on the proportion of the audience feeling unwell, an additional smaller effect of audience size cannot be ruled out.

(ii) Reports of Audience Fainting

When looking in isolation at instances of patrons fainting, reports were again higher in *Titus Andronicus* (overall effect of play: $F_{2,136} = 21.30$, $P < 0.0001$) than in *Julius Caesar* ($P < 0.0001$) and *Antony and Cleopatra* ($P < 0.0001$). The proportion of the audience fainting did not differ significantly between performances of *Antony and Cleopatra* and *Julius Caesar* ($P = 0.19$). When controlling for the influence of other variables, the analysis revealed that audience members were more than twice as likely to fall faint during *Titus Andronicus* as in either of the other two plays. As in (i), the proportion of audience members that fainted was greater on warm/hot days ($F_{1,136} = 16.09$, $P < 0.0001$) and during matinee performances ($F_{1,136} = 5.51$, $P = 0.02$), but no effect of audience size was observed ($F_{1,136} = 1.06$, $P = 0.30$).

References

Shakespeare's Globe Theatre Archive (SGT)

GB 3316 SGT/DEV/EV/202 – Findings from the 1995 Globe Workshop Season Report by Pauline Kiernan, October 1995.

GB 3316 SGT/ED/RES/2/2 – End-of-season interviews, 2006–19.

[1] GB 3316 SGT/ED/RES/2/2/2010/11
[2] GB 3316 SGT/ED/RES/2/2/2011/1
[3] GB 3316 SGT/ED/RES/2/2/2018/2
[4] GB 3316 SGT/ED/RES/2/2/2008/3
[5] GB 3316 SGT/ED/RES/2/2/2009/4
[6] GB 3316 SGT/ED/RES/2/2/2010/6
[7] GB 3316 SGT/ED/RES/2/2/2008/1
[8] GB 3316 SGT/ED/RES/2/2/2010/9
[9] GB 3316 SGT/ED/RES/2/2/2010/7
[10] GB 3316 SGT/ED/RES/2/2/2009/6
[11] GB 3316 SGT/ED/RES/2/2/2009/2
[12] GB 3316 SGT/ED/RES/2/2/2007/1
[13] GB 3316 SGT/ED/RES/2/2/2010/13
[14] GB 3316 SGT/ED/RES/2/2/2010/5
[15] GB 3316 SGT/ED/RES/2/2/2015/1
[16] GB 3316 SGT/ED/RES/2/2/2010/12
[17] GB 3316 SGT/ED/RES/2/2/2019/1
[18] GB 3316 SGT/ED/RES/2/2/2010/8
[19] GB 3316 SGT/ED/RES/2/2/2010/4
[20] GB 3316 SGT/ED/RES/2/2/2008/2
[21] GB 3316 SGT/ED/RES/2/2/2009/3
[22] GB 3316 SGT/ED/RES/2/2/2010/2

[23] GB 3316 SGT/ED/RES/2/2/2010/3
[24] GB 3316 SGT/ED/RES/2/2/2009/5
[25] GB 3316 SGT/ED/RES/2/2/2014/1
[26] GB 3316 SGT/ED/RES/2/2/2019/2

Bailey, Lucy – *Timon of Athens* (dir.), 2008; *Titus Andronicus* (dir.), 2014.

Bertenshaw, Michael – *All's Well That Ends Well*, 2011.

Bushell, Kirsty – *Romeo and Juliet*, 2017.

Butler, Graham – *Henry V*, 2012.

Coy, Jolyon – *Antony and Cleopatra*, 2014.

Cullen, Jonathan – *Doctor Faustus*, 2011.

Dee, Janie – *All's Well That Ends Well*, 2011.

Doel, Imogen – *The Taming of the Shrew*, 2016.

Dromgoole, Dominic – *King Lear* (dir.), 2008.

Edwards, Charles – *Much Ado About Nothing*, 2011.

Flynn, Matthew – *Henry V*, 2012.

Garnon, James – *All's Well That Ends Well*, 2011.

Mann, Jake – *Titus Andronicus*, 2014.

Marcell, Joseph – *Much Ado About Nothing*, 2011.

Monaghan, Jack – *As You Like It*, 2015.

Munby, Jonathan – *A Midsummer Night's Dream* (dir.), 2008.

Nadarajah, Nadia – *Globe Ensemble*, 2018.

Needham, Matthew – *Titus Andronicus*, 2014.

Rosheuvel, Golda – *Romeo and Juliet*, 2017.

Saba, Sirine – *Antony and Cleopatra*, 2014.

Schlesinger, Helen – *Globe Ensemble*, 2018.

Shelford, Gary – *As You Like It*, 2015.

Terry, Michelle – *As You Like It*, 2015.

Wynter, Danny Lee – *King Lear*, 2008.

GB 3316 SGT/THTR/SR/2014 – Show reports for 2014 season.

GB 3316 SGT/THTR/SR/2021 – Show reports for 2021 season.

Holmes, Sean, and Prime Isaacs. 'Meet the Director – *A Midsummer Night's Dream*', internal interview, 7 May 2021.

Ince, Ola, and Rachel Lemon. 'Meet the Director – *Romeo and Juliet*', internal interview, 21 June 2021.

O'Hea, Brendan, and Vanessa Faye-Stanley. 'Meet the Director – Globe on Tour', internal interview, 4 June 2021.

SGT/COMM/PUB/1/11/2 – 'A Culture of Revenge', *Titus Andronicus* programme interview with Lucy Bailey, 2006, pp. 14–15.

SGT/THTR/SM/1/2021/MND (2 boxes) – Production notes, *A Midsummer Night's Dream* (2021).

'A Midsummer Night's Dream 2021 – Covid Specific RA', April 2020.

'Principles of Covid Safe Rehearsing/Performing', 2 March 2020.

Online Resources

Royal Shakespeare Company (RSC). 'Press Release: Shakespeare Still Has Power to Shock – RSC *Titus Andronicus* Audience Research Project Results'. 26 October 2017. www.rsc.org.uk/press/releases/shakespeare-still-has-power-to-shock—-rsc-titus-andronicus-audience-research-project-results.

Shakespeare's Globe. 'Announcing Summer 2021 at the Globe'. Blog. 24 March 2021. www.shakespearesglobe.com/discover/blogs-and-features/2021/03/24/announcing-summer-2021-at-the-globe/.

'Shakespeare's Globe in Lockdown: One Year Later'. Blog. 18 March 2021. www.shakespearesglobe.com/discover/blogs-and-features/2021/03/18/shakespeares-globe-in-lockdown-one-year-later/.

'Press Release: Globe Announces New Digital Content, Free Films, Mark Rylance's Shakespeare Walks, and Online Support for

Students'. 30 March 2020. https://cdn.shakespearesglobe.com/uploads/2020/03/Press-Release-SGT-Digital-Content-for-Isolation-FINAL.pdf.

'Press Release: Shakespeare's Globe Announces the Return of Standing Tickets'. 19 July 2021. https://cdn.shakespearesglobe.com/uploads/2021/07/Press-Release-Shakespeares-Globe-Announces-the-Return-of-Standing-Tickets.pdf.

'Thought of the Week: Remember Thee!'. Blog. 13 June 2020. www.shakespearesglobe.com/discover/blogs-and-features/2020/06/13/thought-of-the-week-remember-thee/.

'Thought of the Week: The Power of the Mind'. Blog. 17 April 2020. www.shakespearesglobe.com/discover/blogs-and-features/2020/04/17/thought-of-the-week-the-power-of-the-mind/.

'Thought of the Week: The Readiness Is All'. Blog. 29 May 2020. www.shakespearesglobe.com/discover/blogs-and-features/2020/05/29/thought-of-the-week-the-readiness-is-all/.

'*Twelfth Night*: Visual Story'. 2021. https://cdn.shakespearesglobe.com/uploads/2021/09/Visual-Story-Twelfth-Night-2021.pdf.

Other Works

Adorno, Theodor. 'The Essay as Form'. *New German Critique*, Spring–Summer, no. 32, 1984: 151–71.

Aebischer, Pascale. *Viral Shakespeare: Performance in the Time of Pandemic*. Cambridge: Cambridge University Press, 2021.

Aebischer, Pascale, and Rachael Nicholas. *Digital Theatre Transformation: A Case Study and Digital Toolkit*. Oxford: Creation Theatre, 2020.

Ahmed, Sara. *The Promise of Happiness*. Durham, NC: Duke University Press, 2010.

À Kempis, Thomas. *Of the Imitation of Christ*, trans. Thomas Rogers. London: printed by Henry Denham, 1580.

Alford, Lucy. *Forms of Poetic Attention*. New York: Columbia University Press, 2020.

Allred, Gemma Kate, Benjamin Broadribb, and Erin Sullivan, eds. *Lockdown Shakespeare: New Evolutions in Performance*. London: Bloomsbury Arden Shakespeare, 2022.

Banks, Fiona, ed. *Shakespeare: Actors and Audiences*. London: Bloomsbury, 2018.

Bar, Moshe. *Mindwandering: How It Can Improve Your Mood and Boost Your Creativity*. London: Bloomsbury, 2022.

Barthes, Roland. *The Neutral: Lecture Course at the Collège de France, 1977– 1978*, trans. Rosalind E. Krauss and Dennis Hollier. New York: Columbia University Press, 2005.

Bell, Julia. *Radical Attention*. London: Peninsula Press, 2020.

Bevis, Matthew. 'In Search of Distraction'. *Poetry*, vol. 211, no. 2, 2017: 171–94.

Billington, Michael. 'To Hear or Not to Hear'. *The Guardian*, 15 June 2000.

Blesser, Barry, and Linda-Ruth Salter. *Spaces Speak, Are You Listening? Experiencing Aural Architecture*. Cambridge, MA: MIT Press, 2009.

Böhme, Gernot. *Atmospheric Architectures: The Aesthetics of Felt Spaces*, trans. A.-Chr. Engles-Schwarzpaul. London: Bloomsbury, 2017.

Brennan, Teresa. *The Transmission of Affect*. Ithaca, NY: Cornell University Press, 2004.

Brown, Mark. 'Shakespeare's Globe to Reopen in May Staging Plays with No Intervals'. *The Guardian*, 24 March 2021.

Burrows, Ian. *Shakespeare for Snowflakes: On Slapstick and Sympathy*. Winchester: Zero Books, 2020.

Carson, Christie, and Farah Karim-Cooper, eds. *Shakespeare's Globe: A Theatrical Experiment*. Cambridge: Cambridge University Press, 2008.

Clark, Nick. 'Globe Theatre Takes Out 100 Audience Members with Its Gory Titus Andronicus'. *The Independent*, 22 July 2014.

Conkie, Rob. 'The Archive: Show Reporting Shakespeare', in *The Arden Research Handbook of Shakespeare and Contemporary Performance*. Peter Kirwan and Kathryn Prince, eds. London: Bloomsbury Arden Shakespeare, 2021, pp. 25–37.

Cook, Amy. 'Cognitive Interplay: How Blending Theory and Cognitive Science Reread Shakespeare', in *Stylistics and Shakespeare's Language: Transdisciplinary Approaches*. Jonathan Culpeper and Mireille Ravassat, eds. London: Bloomsbury, 2011, pp. 246–68.

Cotterill, Anne. *Digressive Voices in Early Modern English Literature*. Oxford: Oxford University Press, 2004.

Dawson, Anthony B. 'The Distracted Globe', in *The Culture of Playgoing in Shakespeare's England: A Collaborative Debate*. Anthony B. Dawson and Paul Yachnin, eds. Cambridge: Cambridge University Press, 2001, pp. 88–107.

Deleuze, Gilles. *The Logic of Sense*, trans. Constantin V. Boundas, Mark Lester, and Charles J. Stivale. London: Bloomsbury, 2015.

Derrida, Jacques. *On the Name*, trans. Thomas Dutoit. Stanford, CA: Stanford University Press, 1995.

Downame, John. *A Guide to Godlynesse*. London: printed by Felix Kingstone, 1622.

Dryden, John, trans. *Plutarch's Lives*. London: printed by T. Hodgkin, 1683.

Dugan. Holly. '"As Dirty as Smithfield and as Stinking Every Whit": The Smell of the Hope Theatre', in *Shakespeare's Theatres and the Effects of Performance*. Farah Karim-Cooper and Tiffany Stern, eds. London: Bloomsbury Arden Shakespeare, 2014, pp. 195–213.

Dustagheer, Sarah. 'Original Practices: Old Ways and New Directions', in *The Arden Research Handbook of Shakespeare and Contemporary Performance*. Peter Kirwan and Kathryn Prince, eds. London: Bloomsbury Arden Shakespeare, 2021, pp. 65–81.

Escolme, Bridget. *Talking to the Audience: Shakespeare, Performance, Self.* London: Routledge, 2005.

 'Being Good: Actors' Testimonies as Archive and the Cultural Construction of Success in Performance'. *Shakespeare Bulletin*, vol. 28, no. 1, 2010: 77–91.

Eyal, Nir. *Indistractable: How to Control Your Attention and Choose Your Life.* London: Bloomsbury, 2019.

Freedman, Barbara. *Staging the Gaze: Postmodernism, Psychoanalysis, and Shakespearean Comedy.* Ithaca, NY: Cornell University Press, 1991.

Gardner, Lyn. 'Titus Andronicus Review'. *The Guardian*, 11 May 2014.

Goldberg, Jonathan. *The Seeds of Things: Theorizing Sexuality and Materiality in Renaissance Representation.* New York: Fordham University Press, 2009.

Granada, Luis de. *Of Prayer and Meditation*, trans. Richard Hopkins. Paris: printed by Thomas Brumeau, 1582.

Greenblatt, Stephen. *Shakespearean Negotiations: The Circulation of Social Energy in Renaissance England.* Oxford: Clarendon Press, 1988.

 The Swerve: How the World Became Modern. New York: W. W. Norton, 2011.

Griffero, Tonino. *Atmospheres: Aesthetics of Emotional Spaces*, trans. Sarah de Sanctis. Farnham: Ashgate, 2014.

 Quasi-Things: The Paradigm of Atmospheres, trans. Sarah de Sanctis. New York: State University of New York Press, 2017.

Hari, Johann. *Stolen Focus: Why You Can't Pay Attention.* London: Bloomsbury, 2022.

Heim, Caroline. *Audience as Performer: The Changing Role of Theatre Audiences in the Twenty-First Century.* London: Routledge, 2015.

Hemming, Sarah. 'Titus Andronicus, Shakespeare's Globe, London – Review'. *Financial Times*, 2 May 2014.

Hodgdon, Barbara. 'Shopping in the Archives: Material Memories', in *Shakespeare, Memory and Performance*. Peter Holland, ed. Cambridge: Cambridge University Press, 2006, pp. 135–67.

Johns, Dani. 'It's No Joke – Since Lockdown, Live Audiences Have Forgotten How to Behave'. *The Guardian*, 21 April 2022.

Johnson, Ryan J. *The Deleuze-Lucretius Encounter*. Edinburgh: Edinburgh University Press, 2016.

Karim-Cooper, Farah. 'Shakespeare's War on Terror: Critical Review of Shakespeare's *Titus Andronicus* (Directed by Lucy Bailey) at Shakespeare's Globe, London, 2006)'. *Shakespeare*, vol 4, no. 1 (2008): 63–71.

Karremann, Isabel. *The Drama of Memory in Shakespeare's History Plays*. Cambridge: Cambridge University Press, 2015.

Kenny, Amy. '"I Hope 'Twill Make You Laugh": Audience Laughter at the Globe Theatre'. *Research International*, vol. 40, no. 1, 2015: 37–49.

Kiernan, Pauline. *Staging Shakespeare at the New Globe*. Basingstoke: Macmillan, 1999.

Kirwan, Peter. 'Titus Andronicus @ Shakespeare's Globe'. *The Bardathon*, 4 July 2014.

Kirwan, Peter, and Erin Sullivan. 'Shakespeare in Lockdown (Review)'. *Shakespeare Bulletin*, vol. 38, no. 3, 2020: 489–93.

Korducki, Kelli María. 'I Have "Pandemic Brain". Will I Ever Be Able to Concentrate Again?'. *The Guardian*, 24 June 2021.

Langley, Eric. *Shakespeare's Contagious Sympathies: Ill Communications*. Oxford: Oxford University Press, 2018.

'The Path to Which Wild Error Leads: A Lucretian *Comedy of Errors*'. *Textual Practice*, vol. 28, no. 2, 2014: 161–87.

Lennox, Gabrielle, and Hannah Mason. 'Virtual *Dream* Reality Check: A Case of Interactive Digital Theatre from the Royal Shakespeare Company'. *Body, Space & Technology*, vol. 22, no. 1, 2022: 1–9.

Leo, John. *A Geographical Historie of Africa*. London: printed by George Bishop, 1600.

Lewis, Rhodri. *Hamlet and the Vision of Darkness*. Princeton, NJ: Princeton University Press, 2020.

Loftis, Sonia Freedman. *Shakespeare and Disability Studies*. Oxford: Oxford University Press, 2021.

Lucretius. *The Nature of Things*, trans. A. E. Stallings. London: Penguin, 2007.

Lyne, Raphael. 'Shakespeare and the Wandering Mind'. *Journal of the British Academy*, vol. 8, 2020: 1–27.

Mason, Robert. *Reasons Academie*. London: printed by Thomas Creede, 1605.

McConachie, Bruce. *Engaging Audiences: A Cognitive Approach to Spectating in the Theatre*. New York: Palgrave Macmillan, 2008.

Miller, Gemma. 'Review of Shakespeare's *Hamlet* and *As You Like It* (directed by Federay Holmes and Elle While for the Globe Ensembles) at Shakespeare's Globe, London, 29 April and 30 May 2018'. *Shakespeare*, vol. 15, no. 1, 2019: 69–72.

Montaigne, Michel de. *Essais*, trans. John Florio. London: printed by Valentine Simmes, 1603.

Neely, Carol Thomas. *Distracted Subjects: Madness and Gender in Shakespeare and Early Modern Culture*. Ithaca, NY: Cornell University Press, 2004.

North, Paul. *The Problem of Distraction*. Stanford, CA: Stanford University Press, 2012.

O'Malley, Evelyn. *Weathering Shakespeare: Audiences and Open-Air Performance*. London: Bloomsbury, 2020.

Orman, Steve. 'Titus Andronicus (Shakespeare's Globe)'. *Blogging Shakespeare*, 31 May 2014.

Pangallo, Matteo, and Peter Kirwan, eds. *Shakespeare's Audiences*. London: Routledge, 2021.

Petrarch. *Phisicke against Fortune, aswell Prosperous, as Aduerse Conteyned in Two Bookes*, trans. Thomas Twyne. London: printed by Thomas Dawson, 1579.

Phillips, Adam. *Attention Seeking*. London: Penguin, 2019.

Purcell, Stephen. 'Performing the Public at Shakespeare's Globe'. *Shakespeare*, vol. 14, no. 1, 2018: 51–63.

Shakespeare and Audience in Practice. Basingstoke: Palgrave Macmillan, 2013.

Renel, William. 'Sonic Accessibility: Increasing Social Equity through the Inclusive Design of Sound in Museums and Heritage Sites'. *Curator: The Museum Journal*, vol. 62, no. 3, 2019: 377–402.

Sartre, Jean-Paul. *Sartre on Theatre*, trans. Frank Jellinek. Michel Contat and Michel Rybalka, eds. New York: Pantheon, 1976.

Sedgman, Kirsty. *The Reasonable Audience: Theatre Etiquette, Behaviour Policing, and the Live Performance Experience*. Basingstoke: Palgrave Macmillan, 2018.

Serres, Michel. *The Birth of Physics*, trans. David Webb and William Ross. London: Rowman & Littlefield International, 2018.

Shakespeare, William. *Hamlet*, rev. ed. Ann Thompson and Neil Taylor, eds. London: Bloomsbury Arden Shakespeare, 2016.

The Norton Shakespeare, 3rd ed. Stephen Greenblatt, Walter Cohen, Suzanne Gossett et al., eds. New York: W. W. Norton, 2017.

Shaughnessy, Robert. 'Connecting the Globe: Actors, Audiences and Entrainment'. *Shakespeare Survey*, vol. 68, 2015: 294–305.

Shirilan, Stephanie. 'Respiratory Sympathy and Pneumatic Community in Shakespeare', in *Shakespeare's Audiences*. Matteo Pangallo and Peter Kirwan, eds. London: Routledge, 2021, pp. 27–44.

Smith, Bruce. *The Acoustic World of Early Modern England: Attending to the O-Factor*. Chicago, IL: University of Chicago Press, 1999.

Snapes, Laura. 'Musicians Want Us to Pay Closer Attention at Gigs. Let's Do Them the Courtesy'. *The Guardian*, 21 April 2022.

Stillman, Anne. 'Distraction Fits'. *Thinking Verse*, II, 2012: 27–69.

Sullivan, Erin. 'Live to Your Living Room: Streamed Theatre, Audience Experience, and the Globe's *A Midsummer Night's Dream*'. *Participants: Journal of Audience & Reception Studies*, vol. 17, no. 1, 2020: 92–119.

    'Immersion in a Time of Deep Distraction', in *Lockdown Shakespeare: New Evolutions in Performance*. Gemma Kate Allred, Benjamin Broadribb, and Erin Sullivan, eds. London: Bloomsbury Arden Shakespeare, 2022, pp. 107–26.

Tosh, Will. *Playing Indoors: Staging Early Modern Drama in the Sam Wanamaker Playhouse*. London: Bloomsbury Arden Shakespeare, 2018.

Tribble, Evelyn B. *Cognition in the Globe: Attention and Memory in Shakespeare's Theatre*. Basingstoke: Palgrave Macmillan, 2011.

    'Dropping Like flies: Skilled Coordination and Front-of-House at Shakespeare's Globe', in *Collaborative Embodied Performance: Ecologies of Skill*. Kath Bicknell and John Sutton, eds. London: Bloomsbury Methuen Drama, 2022, pp. 21–34.

Tripney, Natasha. 'Lucy Bailey: "It Takes a Wild Approach to Release a Play's Energy"'. *The Stage*, 20 November 2015.

Warner, Marina. 'There's Method in Theatre's Blood and Gore'. *The Guardian*, 12 May 2014.

Webster, John. 'An Excellent Actor', in *Sir Thomas Overbury his Wife*. London: printed by Edward Griffin, 1616, M2r-M3r.

West, William N. *Common Understandings, Poetic Confusion: Playhouses and Playgoers in Elizabethan England*. Chicago, IL: University of Chicago Press, 2021.

Widley, George. *The Doctrine of the Sabbath*. London: printed by Felix Kingstone, 1604.

Williams, David. 'Weather'. *Performance Research*, vol. 11, no. 3, 2006: 142–4.

Williams, Holly. 'Titus Andronicus, Shakespeare's Globe, Theatre Review'. *The Independent*, 2 May 2014.

Wood, Michael. 'Distraction Theory: How to Read While Thinking of Something Else'. *Michigan Quarterly Review*, vol. XLVIII, no. 4, 2009: 577–88.

Woodall, James. '10 Questions for Director Lucy Bailey'. *The Arts Desk*, 26 October 2016.

Woods, Penelope. 'Audiences at the Old Globe and the New', in *The Cambridge Guide to the Worlds of Shakespeare*, Vol. 2 The World's Shakespeare, 1660–Present. Bruce R. Smith and Katherine Rowe, eds. Cambridge: Cambridge University Press, 2016, pp. 1538–44.

'Globe Audiences: Spectatorship and Reconstruction at Shakespeare's Globe', PhD Thesis. Queen Mary University of London and Shakespeare's Globe, 2012.

Worthen, W. B. *Shakespeare and the Force of Modern Performance*. Cambridge: Cambridge University Press, 2003.

'Interactive, Immersive and Original Shakespeare'. *Shakespeare Bulletin*, vol. 35, no. 3, 2017: 407–24.

Zhao, Sijia, Kengo Shibata, Peter J. Hellyer et al. 'Rapid Vigilance and Episodic Memory Decrements in COVID-19 Survivors'. *Brain Communications*, vol. 4, no. 1, 2022: fcab295.

Acknowledgements

I am grateful to Bill Worthen and the anonymous readers of this Element for their encouraging feedback, and to Pascale Aebischer for her enthusiasm for this work at proposal stage. I would like to thank the extended Globe family, particularly Victoria Lane and Mel Chetwood, who went above and beyond in providing me with access to the Globe archive, as well as the actors and directors who gave their time to the Research department for these interviews (special thanks to Michelle Terry and Sophie Russell for their personal interviews). This little book simply would not have been possible without them. I would also like to express my gratitude to Cambridge University Press (in particular Adam Hooper, Emily Hockley, and the typesetters) for their patience with various formatting requests, and to Tristram Kenton, Pete Le May, and William Renel for image permissions. Thank you to the friends and colleagues who have discussed various aspects of this project with me – Richard Ashby, Hailey Bachrach, Rebecca Beasely, Ursula Clayton, Deyasini Dasgupta, Jonathan Green, John Gulledge, Laurie Maguire, Kathryn Murphy, Stephen Purcell, Macs Smith, and my students at Queen's – to Josh Garrod for reading this stuff again and again, and to Eric Langley for shaping so much of my thinking here. And, finally, thank you to Farah Karim-Cooper and Will Tosh, who have supported this project from the very beginning - this Element is dedicated to them.

Cambridge Elements ≡

Shakespeare Performance

W. B. Worthen
Barnard College

W. B. Worthen is Alice Brady Pels Professor in the Arts, and
Chair of the Theatre Department at Barnard College. He is also
co-chair of the Ph.D. Program in Theatre at Columbia University,
where he is Professor of English and Comparative Literature.

ABOUT THE SERIES

Shakespeare Performance is a dynamic collection in a field that is both always emerging and always evanescent. Responding to the global range of Shakespeare performance today, the series launches provocative, urgent criticism for researchers, graduate students and practitioners. Publishing scholarship with a direct bearing on the contemporary contexts of Shakespeare performance, it considers specific performances, material and social practices, ideological and cultural frameworks, emerging and significant artists and performance histories.

Cambridge Elements ⹀

Shakespeare Performance

A full series listing is available at: www.cambridge.org/ESPF

Printed in the United States
by Baker & Taylor Publisher Services